THE DOs & DON'Ts OF PARENTING ADULT KIDS

PRACTICAL WAYS TO KEEP YOUR
RELATIONSHIP HEALTHY AND
LONG-LASTING, EVEN WHEN
CHALLENGES ARISE

ANN MARIE SORENSON

The Do's and Don'ts of Parenting Adult Kids: Practical Ways to Keep Your Relationship Healthy and Long-Lasting, Even When Challenges Arise ©2023 by Ann Marie Sorenson

This book contains the opinions and ideas of its author. It is intended to provide helpful and informative material on the subject addressed within. The material is offered with the understanding that the author is not engaging in rendering medical, health, mental health, legal services, or any other kind of professional services. Readers should consult their medical, health, mental health, legal, or other competent professionals before adopting any of the suggestions in this book or drawing inferences from the material.

The author specifically disclaims all responsibility for any liability, loss, or risk, personal or otherwise, which is incurred as a consequence, directly or indirectly, of the use and application of any of the contents of this book.

Dedicated to my beautiful daughters who brought joy, purpose, and love into my life.

— A. M. S.

CONTENTS

INTRODUCTION

Me? Write a book? Never! But here I am, and yes, I did! In retrospect, it's not unusual for me to do something I never dreamed of doing, and it's often when I'm not even looking for it. I recently retired from teaching, and now I am busy with my real estate career and substitute teaching. But when I stumbled across an online course for "newbie" writers and publishers, I dove right in, and I'm so glad I did.

Jon, my loving husband, was diagnosed with cancer on September 17, 2020, and passed away on September 11, 2021. I am grateful for that year we had together. We engaged in heartfelt conversations and would reminisce into the night, remembering fond memories we had during our 35-year marriage. Our daughters, Karina and Shawna, were also at our house often, spending quality time with him, helping him run his business, running errands, as well as laughing and crying with him. They shared candid moments and some of the hurts they experienced while growing up. We could finally speak openly about things that were just too difficult to think about before. It was as if healing was bestowed upon us by the Lord.

When I became a widow, I had time to reflect on our marriage, what we did right as parents, and where we dropped the ball. The teenage years into early adulthood with our girls were the most difficult; not-so-great boyfriends, partying, expulsion from high school, moving out, college and career choices, arguments, needing money, car accidents, trips to the ER, a pregnancy, and the list goes on. Jon and I were frustrated, tired, and clueless as to how to help them while trying to maintain our sanity. But with prayer, counseling, and hard work, God was faithful.

Now my daughters are in their mid-30s, and both are happily married with families of their own. The challenges we have are still there, just different; husbands, grandkids, stepkids, in-laws, holidays, vacations, and other sensitive subjects. How involved should I be in their lives? When do I speak up or shut up? How do I help but not enable? And now that Jon is no longer here, our lives have changed. I felt that maybe, just maybe, I could be a part of something bigger than myself. Parenting adult children is something millions of us are doing, and we could use a little (or a lot of) help along the way. In preparation for this book, I did extensive research and read a number of books and articles from renowned psychologists, clinical therapists, professors, and parents. I watched countless interviews with experts on this subject. I joined some groups on social media that include parents struggling with difficult and toxic adult kids. As an elementary teacher for 22 years, I listened to parents and grandparents share their hopes and fears for their kids and grandkids. Many spoke candidly about their family traumas and pain.

Healthy relationships are what we long for and work hard to protect, but we all know there are bumps in the road, big bumps, and little bumps. Oftentimes, situations pop up that blindside us, leaving us wondering, "What now?" Every family is unique with their triumphs and trials. I wrote this book for me as much as for you. "I wish I knew then what I know now" runs through my mind as I discover new nuggets of wisdom, and I know you will find them too. The chapters in this book offer sound, common-sense solutions to complicated issues. There may be some "dos and don'ts" that you may question or not agree with, and that's ok. You will also realize that some things don't apply and that you're doing great in a particular area. Other things you read will speak profoundly to your situation, giving you the confidence to take a different approach or make a healthier decision for you and your adult child. Facing the truth and dealing with it is the beginning of positive change. So trust your instincts, pray, and connect with others that you respect and trust.

When it comes to relationships, especially in families, it's never a "one size fits all" approach. My daughters couldn't be more opposite in their personalities, temperaments, and tastes. One is quiet and internalizes her feelings and emotions. The other is quite chatty and has no problem expressing her feelings and emotions. As parents, although we love our kids equally, we understand that they each have their individual uniqueness, and so we adjust our parenting style accordingly. This holds true whether they are 4 or 40.

One of the best things I did recently was reach out to a family therapist whom I now see twice a month. Hannah has keen insight into relationships, boundaries, trauma, and childhood wounds. She has the ability to shed light on areas that are hidden or suppressed. I'm learning to trust and validate myself, which I couldn't do as a child. I realize that I carried learned behaviors from my childhood and manifested those as a wife and parent. Some were healthy and loving. Others were harmful and destructive. Yes, we are human and have all fallen short in the parenting department, but being honest and accepting our mistakes is necessary for staying close and connected to our kids.

My kids are adults now. Yours might be happy, well-adjusted, and thriving, or they might be immature, selfish, failing to launch, or toxic. Estrangement between parents and their adult kids is more common these days and is often referred to as the "silent epidemic. You might be experiencing that in your own life. Sometimes the relationship improves over time, but unfortunately, in many cases, it doesn't. Our kids have choices, and those choices may leave us devastated. You can learn to let go, live a full, productive life, and love them, in spite of their behavior.

My hope is that you will continue being the caring, loving parent that you are while discovering new ways to share life with your adult child. You're not alone, and I trust this book will give you encouragement and new perspectives. There are practical strategies that we can start using today to help our kids and us. Remember, we are human. God loves us and is for us.

If any of you lacks wisdom, you should ask God, who gives generously to all without finding fault, and it will be given to you. — *James 1:5*

The Dos and Don'ts of Parenting Adult Kids

CHAPTER ONE

DO OPEN YOUR EYES TO THE CHANGING CULTURE, DON'T DOUBT YOUR INSTINCTS

Fun fact: Parenting is hard!

From diapers to drivers, your kids will never stop being your kids, and you will never stop being a parent.

As a mother of two adults, Karina and Shawna, the ups and downs of navigating our relationship have added their fair share of grey hair on my head. It's easy enough to insert yourself into your kids' lives when they're young. But... getting involved and keeping in touch gets a lot tougher the older they get.

I wrote this book for parents wading into the unknown and tricky waters of dealing with adult children. I've been there, done that, and am still there doing that.

I'd like to believe that my years of experience dealing with crises and events have equipped me with the wisdom of the lived and experienced. Let the amicable nature of relations I have with my kids be a testament to a job well done.

God knows I've had my fair share of challenges, but I've risen from them stronger and better every time, and so can you. While subjective experience may differ from person to person, certain experiences are human and universal.

In this chapter, let's look at why these differences might crop up, how a significant cultural shift is taking place, and begin on our journey to see how we could deal with such issues.

We can start working on them in earnest by spelling them out and bringing them out to the light.

The Adult Child Has Become Someone I Don't Know

Your kids may have your nose, your spouse's smile, and ears, but as they grow older, you will slowly realize you may not know them anymore. For instance, a family I know of with a very strict stance on homosexuality was shocked one morning when their adult son came out to them and told them he was moving out to live with his boyfriend. Their initial shock soon led to disappointment, and they began to wonder, 'where did we go wrong?'

Despite how hard parents might try to inculcate certain values into kids when they're young, things cannot (and often don't) always go as planned. Kids may drop out of college, have a child out of wedlock, get arrested for drinking and driving, or get into other precarious situations. My youngest daughter found herself pregnant at 20 and not having the slightest clue what her life would look like. I reassured her that her dad and I would be there for her and her baby but kept our concerns and opinions to ourselves. A beautiful baby boy was born, and Mom and Dad were married a few months later.

In addition to these major events, there are more subtle differences and values that your kids have not picked up from you, which may strain and impact your relationship. For example, many families have been torn apart by sensitive topics like politics, social issues, and sexuality. While such might be the case, the *where did I go wrong* narrative should, in most instances, be disregarded. Just because they do not share the same values as you do, does not necessarily mean you have failed. Their actions and decisions cannot be taken as an accurate measure of your failure or success as a parent! That said, if you hope to foster a positive relationship with them despite these events, these actions would require an appropriate response and a reaction.

First things first, I always make it a point to get down on my knees and pray. Trust God to give you peace and direction. Do not allow the bitterness to fester, and address it as soon as possible. When facing such dilemmas, reaching out to trusted family members, friends, church groups, professionals, and online support groups can be of great comfort. Sharing your hurts, anger, or confusion helps you come to terms with your situation and reminds you that you are not alone. By seeking advice from others, you can compound strategies to reconcile with your family situation. They can help provide solutions on how to adapt to this new normal.

After the prayers have been said and the counseling has been done, now comes the tough part: communicating with your child. You need not compromise your convictions and beliefs to have a civil conversation with them. They are now adults capable of making their own decisions and dealing with the consequences of said decisions. Know that you did all you could, and at all times, be sure to keep communication lines open. You may have your differences, but the fact that you picked up this book tells me you still love them. Let them know this too!

For you create my inmost being; you knit me together in my mother's womb. I praise you because I am fearfully and wonderfully made; your works are wonderful, I know that full well.
— Psalm 139: 13,14

The Generation Gap

Here is a closer look at our differing generations, as well as the cultural changes our kids have and are experiencing. If we can better understand the world they are growing up in, then hopefully, we will see how their environment influences their personality, decisions, and beliefs.

Baby boomers, born between 1946 and 1960, kept relationships at the forefront as they were not impacted by technology while growing up. They, like myself, grew up in an era when phone calls and writing letters were a way to keep in touch. These days, it's almost impossible to get through life without knowing how to use a computer or cell phone. Those born between 1960 and 1979 make up the Generation X, right after the baby boomers. They saw the rise of computer access and used technology more for information and work to boost their productivity. Millennials, or Generation Y, refers to those born between 1980 and 1996. This group has grown up with heavy internet usage, cell phones, apps, and significant technological advancements. My kids and grandkids are naturally "techy" and know so much more than I do about anything phone, tv, or computer related. These distinct generations contribute to differences in value systems and how these adults navigate their way through the world. This chart helps to distinguish between the generations we are discussing. No matter what group you, your children, or your grandchildren fall under, these generations are quite unique and reveal major differences in the way we view the world around us. This chart helps to identify some characteristics of each generation:

	BABY BOOMERS	GENERATION X	GENERATION Y
VALUES	Personal Growth Team work Personal Uniqueness Personal gratification	Self-reliance Autonomy Independence Entrepreneurship Diversity	Honesty Integrity Diversity Responsibility Team work
CHARACTERISTICS	Individualistic Competitive Materialistic Relationship focused Team player Sensitive to feedback Respectful of authority	Comfortable with change Cynical Pragmatic Flexible Multi-tasking Creative Resourceful Autonomous Goal-oriented	Social Confident Optimistic Achievement oriented Co-operative Educated Tech Socially aware Altruistic Multi-tasking Practical Team worker
WORK PREFERENCES	Job-focused "Live to work" mentality Job security Power Career progression	Career focused Work life balance Lack of job security Informal approach to work	Meaningful work Flexible work Mentoring/Feedback Career Focused

Let's focus on the millennials since most of our adult kids are in this generation. They have been labeled the "Me" generation, displaying more selfish, individualistic behaviors. Author, Stephanie Kramer, addresses the correlation between millennials and narcissism in her article, *Stuck on Yourself: Are Millennials Really More Individualistic?*

> "The traditional image of a narcissist is familiar: someone gazing at themselves in the mirror and falling in love with their own reflection. But narcissism is a bit more complex than mere vanity. It can be a serious psychological issue, and those affected might not always be readily willing to seek help. So, what actually makes a narcissist? The word

is used so often nowadays that you might think:

Is narcissism really on the rise? Judging by the number of books written on the topic in recent years, it's hard to resist the idea. Some psychologists say that millennials (those born between 1981 and 1996), influenced by cultural changes like the rise of the internet, are more self-obsessed and narcissistic than previous generations. They say that 20-somethings are more individualistic and concerned with themselves than any generations before them.

Others, just as strongly, oppose the view that millennials are individualistic. Millennials are more diverse, more educated, and more single than earlier generations. But are they also more narcissistic? If they are, what does that mean for the future of society and the world?

The alarm sounded more than a decade ago by some researchers about "millennials being narcissistic" has long since become mainstream. Among them is Dr. Jean Twenge, a psychologist at San Diego State University, who has published several books on the subject.

Twenge claims that modern culture is moving toward greater individualism and has produced a generation of young people with overinflated egos. On NPR's *Hidden Brain* podcast, Twenge argues that social media is a driving force behind the trend, as it encourages constant self-promotion and enables people to broadcast every detail of their lives. At the same time, parenting styles have fostered increased levels of self-esteem and a sense of specialness.

Everyone belongs to his or her generation. The culture you grow up in, along with economic and world events as well as behavioral norms, shape your worldview. In general, says Twenge, millennials see themselves in a more positive light, have high expectations, and are less attuned to global events."

It is apparent that many parents nowadays are struggling with issues they have with their Millennial child. I have read countless stories and spoken with many distraught parents in which the relationship is either on life support or non-existent. "My child isn't even speaking to me!" they say. If you are one of those parents, I truly can identify and care about what you are going through. I hope and pray healing will occur. In the meantime, keep praying and don't give up (more on that in chapter 6).

Let's remember that our thoughts, attitudes, and beliefs directly affect how we relate to our kids, no matter their age. Both parties must come to understand that they are different. But rather than seeing this difference as a stumbling block to their relationship, working on making the best of their situation by communicating honestly and consciously while not disregarding the other opinion becomes very important. Because our starting points were different, we can be worlds apart when it comes to things like work, money, spending, marriage, raising kids, and travel. Once you acknowledge the differences, you can begin working through them and getting past them.

The Impact of Culture on Families

The family unit is the foundation of any society, so it would be natural to assume that changes in the society's fabric would affect families too. What tampers with this societal fabric, you ask? It's the culture of the people. As might have been evident from the previous paragraph, when a person is born can dramatically affect how they turn out as an adult.

The world we live in today and the perceptions held by the majority are all affected by the society we live in and participate in daily. The news and media we consume, the education we receive, the people we associate with, where we live, the food we eat, and the language we speak constitute this culture's aspects.

These changes can either be negative or positive. One such positive change could be seen in the improved position of women in society. Having two amazing daughters myself, I am glad for the world of opportunities available to them that I might not have been afforded when I was their age. Moving women out of the home has allowed all family members to become more versatile in their job contributions. This being said, research has shown that there has been a significant decrease in women looking to get married, and investment in test tube babies is at an all-time high.

Decreased family sizes and increased mobility have also separated families. One-parent families and quasi-family units based on cohabitation now dominate our society. This has dramatically altered the institution of 'family,' and children are now growing up during a time when culturalization is affecting so many aspects of their lives. Traditional marriage is under attack, and 37% of all marriages end in divorce. Most children go through a difficult time during a divorce, and their physical, psychological, emotional, and intellectual well-being can be affected.

In speaking about the family size, I would like to mention that things are all the more difficult in families where fathers are absent, and not necessarily just in a physical sense. In fact, studies have found that the impact of emotionally unavailable fathers is almost the same as that of a physically absent father. Here are some eye-opening stats found in children raised in a father-absent environment:

1. Exponentially increased rates of depression and anxiety
2. Five times more likely to commit suicide
3. 32 times more prone to incarceration
4. Increased school dropout rates
5. Increased rates of divorce and relationship issues, substance abuse, and social and mental behavioral issues

Family time and recreational activities are also very different from how they used to be. We live in a highly consumerist culture where instant entertainment is easily accessed. While it is easier to keep your kids entertained with screen time, one must ask, at what cost? The internet often exposes them to things they should be kept away from. Culturalization again happens in a manner that leads to kids growing up with increasingly deviant behavior. Things like premarital sex and drug abuse become normalized, which skews their moral perceptions of right and wrong. Of course, obesity and diabetes are also direct consequences of sedentary behavior.

All this might sound rather dreary, but such are the times we live in. The next heading shall look at another major effect of today's societal culture.

Social Media and its Unhealthy Chokehold

The world we live in today is not the same as it was even 30 years ago. The aforementioned technological boom in the Generation Y era has changed our lives. The internet has become an indispensable part of our everyday lives. While some might say this has allowed us to establish stronger connections with those far away, the inverse might be true for those closest to us. Nothing is more isolating than silently sitting in a room with a person staring at their phone screen. Alas, such is often the case these days.

The 'iPad kids' have become an ever-growing category to talk about, as toddlers are given access to technology a wee bit too early. Kids, teens, and young adults spend far too much time playing video games or on apps like Snapchat, TikTok, Instagram, and Youtube. The internet often exposes them to things they should be kept away from. According to a report by Common Sense Media, three-quarters of teens have viewed pornography online by the age of 17, with the average age of first exposure at the age of 12. "Facebook" adults could also be a category of its own to describe adults constantly online, be it for work or leisure. It takes discipline and commitment to stay off our phones and have meaningful interactions and conversations. I'm "guilty as charged" when I, too, find myself scrolling longer than I care to confess. Internet addiction and Screen Dependency Disorder are very real and affect both young and old alike.

Constant engagement with social media has given rise to several studies that show their negative impact on kids and adults alike. Increased screen time affects them not only physically (eye strain, lack of exercise) but also mentally. We can understand why there is a direct correlation between screen time among young people and increased isolation, lack of concentration, depression, self-harm, and suicide. Adults who clock in high levels of screen time have also shown decreased levels of concentration, decreased memory capacity, and also increased levels of depression and loneliness.

Exposure to fast media, like fast food, spoils the mind. If social media happens to be taking up an overwhelming amount of your child's time and is visibly affecting their lifestyle habits and making them less happy individuals or leading them towards a downward spiral, it might be time to take action. We, along with our children and grandchildren, need limits on screen time. I have found that holding each other accountable and developing good habits will make a difference. In addition, informing your adult kids of the consequences of such compulsive media obsessions or sending them well-meaning links to relevant studies might go a long way.

Political, Social, and Identity Issues

Apart from the somewhat-obvious cultural changes and the gap between different generations, there is another kind of divide that is increasingly visible in today's society — political, social, and identity mismatch.

A few days back, I was talking with a few of my long-lost friends. It was a school reunion. After reminiscing about the good old days, the conversation gravitated toward kids, and we soon entered a rabbit hole. My friend, Barbara, was in tears because her son didn't visit them anymore due to political differences. This entire battle of Democrat vs. Republican, Left vs. Right, and Liberal vs. Conservative is not only happening between political leaders, but it is digging a rift in the families, such that it seems almost impossible to heal the divide. It is really difficult to strike the right balance when beliefs and ideals are completely opposite.

This is what recent data show as well. Political diversity is not appreciated as it was in my generation. And there appears to be an ever-widening gap between children and parents. Even couples with opposite political ideologies find it difficult to support each other.

There is not one America now. Each one of us pictures it differently based on our own perceptions, largely framed by our experiences, political preferences, and priorities. It is only natural that finding common ground in a family with differing views is a challenging task to achieve. It is not the first time we have faced choices, and we must pick one of the two. We all have our opinions, not just with kids but also with friends. I remember days when my friends and I would quarrel because two of us wanted to play hide and seek, but the others didn't. We used to conclude amicably and mutually. Growing up, I realized my political views were poles apart from my best friend's. But that's where the beauty lies, no? Homogeneity is overrated. Heterogeneity adds variety and spice to our life. We need to understand that growth lies not in connecting with like-minded people but with ones who challenge our ideologies and make us think about why we support what we support. But reaching this stage needs a lot of maturity and acceptance, and I believe that's what's needed today.

Unsurprisingly, this seems to be a natural manifestation of a society divided on an array of factors and not just politics. Race, economic gaps, ethics, sexual orientation, and gender identity are other "hot topic" issues, to name a few.

The LBGTQ and trans-gender communities have become widely accepted, and laws have been passed to protect those individuals. Our kids are also growing up in a culture where there aren't just two genders but at least 58 gender identities, according to some. Seriously? This is confusing, strange, and difficult for parents, especially if your child identifies as someone completely different than how he/she was raised. I recently met a woman at a Bible study who shared a painful part of her life. Her estranged son had a sex change operation and is now living out of the country. He wants nothing to do with the family, and there has been no contact for many years. She hopes and prays for that phone call from him but accepts the fact that it may never happen.

Many young people have sided with the woke ideology. The term "woke," according to Webster's dictionary, is defined as "aware of and actively attentive to important facts and issues (especially issues of racial and social justice)." This appears to be good and well-intentioned. However, others see them as ultra-sensitive, easily offended, and can't relate to those with differing opinions. I don't like putting labels on anyone or anything, but an unwillingness to have a free exchange of ideas only brings division and undermines healthy relationships.

We watch and read the news, and unfortunately, so much of it is mixed with opinions and ideology. We can take on a certain bias depending on who or what we listen to. Young people especially are more easily influenced, whether it's by peers, education, advertising, and all the media they are exposed to on a daily basis. But for our purposes, loving our adult kids, no matter what they believe or identify as, should be a priority. We were created to love and be loved. God loves us in spite of our choices or lifestyle, and nothing we do will change that. Let us love others with that same unconditional affection.

We do not know the plans God has for our kids' lives. As their parents, we were put on this earth to guide them to the best of our abilities, but we cannot be with them forever. Keep your faith in the hope that our Father in heaven will not let a single sheep go astray. Keep communication lines open and give God a chance to work in your children's and your heart too.

Conclusion

I hope I didn't leave you too discouraged, but the changes we are experiencing in our culture and society are directly impacting our kids and our relationships with them. And yes, sometimes, what we see, hear, and read these days can be "shocking." But the human experience has remained the same since the dawn of creation. I believe we were created for meaningful, lasting relationships. We need God and each other to make us whole, thriving human beings. We will experience pain and frustration in this ever-changing world, but let's not give up on what truly matters. Some major takeaways from this chapter would be as follows:

- Change is inevitable, be it during our parent's time or during our time as a parent. Rather than fighting change, let's learn to see the positives in it and try to understand it. This does not mean you let go of your principles and convictions. It simply means you adopt a more nuanced worldview.
- Remember, the culture our adult kids live in is dramatically different from when we were their age. Family structure, social media, the internet, cell phones, politics, changing values, and shifting norms all play a part in their lifestyle and priorities.
- And last but not least, pray for your kids always. In God's eyes, we are all children. Despite your, theirs, or even my shortcomings, all we can do is entrust them in God's hands.

CHAPTER TWO

DO ADJUST TO YOUR ROLE AS A PARENT, DON'T HOLD ON SO TIGHTLY

How you connect with your children is very different from how your parents might have connected with you. Dealing with adult kids can be very different from dealing with a messy 5-year-old or even a 17-year-old angst adolescent.

Some might even say it's the hardest part of parenting because now you're dealing with a different, fully formed adult individual with his/her own ambitions and goals. It's easy enough to deal with tantrums when you know they're mad because you took their Xbox away for a bad exam result, but how to deal with the "not-so-nice texts, distancing, silence, and awkward Thanksgiving dinners when you don't know what you said wrong and when you misstepped?

This chapter will look at how you can initiate that gear shift from dealing with small children to adult children. It shall look at practical ways to come to terms with these roles as we venture into this new parenting style.

Your expectations may not be theirs

As parents, we naturally encourage our kids to do their best and achieve their goals. As they approach adulthood, we step back and keep cheering them on, but we should have realistic expectations for them. It's easy to project an idealized image of what they should be like. However, you and your child need to understand each other's shortcomings more. By doing this, you will quite frankly not be disappointed as often as you would have been if you harbored high expectations.

Speaking candidly, I expected both my girls to go to college and graduate with a degree, just like their mom. But, although they did some college, they both chose careers in the cosmetology industry. It took me a while to accept this. However, they both love what they do, are highly skilled in their profession, and provide a wonderful service to their clients as an esthetician and a hairdresser, respectively.

Realize that they are adults. You are a friend, not a boss. Anyone above the age of 21 can be considered a full-fledged adult capable of making their own decisions. While it may be tempting to dictate what your child can and cannot do, you are no longer the reigning authority in their life; they are the masters of their own destiny.

As they grow older, the dynamics in your relationship will naturally change. They'll leave the house, go to college, get jobs, and eventually set up their own families. No matter what they do, you will have to recalibrate your relationship in different directions taking into account the types of lives you both now live. Rather than being a boss who nags and tells them what to do, be a friend who listens to their problems and occasionally offers advice.

My honest advice? Relax! You've done what you needed to do! Now let them take responsibility for their actions. This was the area I struggled the most with. When my girls moved out and rented an apartment, I knew things were going on that I didn't approve of. I was always the "hovering" mom, but now I had to let them go, pray for protection, and be there when they needed me. While worrying is a natural parental instinct, you'll soon get used to letting your kid make their own decisions and deal with the consequences, good or bad.

Listen more and talk less

Hearing of your child's pain and trauma - and maybe you have been the one who unintentionally inflicted it - can give rise to many complicated emotions. But what needs to be acknowledged is that your adult child's experience is just as valid as there's ever been.

While some might like to believe that an accusation from our children is simply a matter of their misunderstanding, misinterpretation, or exaggeration, it's important that we hear them out without becoming defensive, getting angry, or freaking out.

Refrain from getting too emotional. An emotionally charged person is more likely to make a mistake they might regret in the coming future. When you're too emotional, you end up interrupting, questioning, attempting to clarify, or denying the incident altogether. Your child might tell you about what hurt them, and your take on the situation might have been completely different, but holding your tongue would be prudent at the moment.

Those who guard their lips preserve their lives [and their relationships], but those who speak rashly will come to ruin.   — *Proverbs 13:3*

If you wish to open more honest communication channels, it would be in your best interest to listen to what they say to you.

Try not to get defensive. An extension of the previous point, make sure not to get a counter-attack. This is not a fight. This is a discussion and a conversation. If they bare their heart and feelings for you, and you reply with a scathing retort that invalidates their experience, you can only imagine the wonders that would do for your already fraying relationship.

Give them affirmation. Ensure that you are listening and appreciate their honesty in communicating their thoughts and feelings with you. By doing so, they might feel more comfortable approaching you more frequently and whenever you have conflicts and issues. The conversation is key, so it should be encouraged.

Ask them if they're willing to listen to a response or if they just want to vent. This will help you better gauge the nature of the situation and allow you to bring your concerns and positions to the forefront. Be sure that when you reply, do not deny, defend, or blame. These could turn interactions sour. That also works if they do not allow you to make your own point. It will show them you care enough about this matter to put their feelings before yours. If the urge to give a reply does not seem to be subsiding, pray! Let all your apprehensions and tensions out before the lord, and your heavy and burdened yoke shall be taken upon his shoulders.

Accept responsibility

Accept responsibility where responsibility is due and ask them for forgiveness if you have transgressed against them. The only way to make any relationship work, not only the one you have with your child, is to be reflexive of your actions and reactions.

As parents, it may be difficult to apologize to your child. And it's not just you. A lot of parents have this belief that they cannot do anything wrong toward their children. Sure, you only want what's best for them. But you're not perfect either, and you have to acknowledge the fact that it's very possible for you to unintentionally do something that can hurt your child.

So, when you see your child distressed, angry, or resentful towards you, ask yourself this – *"Have I done something wrong to make them feel this way? Is their anger or frustration towards me justified?"* And make amends by offering them a heartfelt apology.

Don't be cryptic or beat around the bush when you ask for their forgiveness. Be clear with your words and speak them out loud to them. Tell them you're truly sorry if you've done anything to hurt them. Sometimes, even when you feel like you haven't done anything to apologize, it can still be helpful to say sorry to them if it makes them feel better or eases their mind. Apologizing isn't a sign of weakness but a sign of acceptance and a great way to mend your relationship with them.

And after you've asked for forgiveness, the next important step is communicating. A common issue for parents is that even when they try their best to do everything good for their children, they only see the world from their own eyes and not from the perspective of the children as well. That is why both parent and child must sit down and communicate each other's feelings and points of view.

Speaking honestly, my husband and I were far from perfect parents. And if my husband were alive today, he would agree. When I look back and try connecting the dots, I have to acknowledge that we did project our own issues and trauma into the parenting experience. I have always been the one who preferred peace over arguments because that was the type of home I was raised in. My husband had insecurities about being a good father because he didn't have a healthy role model from his own father. He was present physically but unavailable emotionally. I tried to be both mom and dad, as well as trying to keep my girls happy through the dysfunction.

It wasn't until years later that Jon and I both realized our mistakes, and our girls communicated that to us very clearly. They both wished we had given them more chores and responsibilities because they had difficulty adjusting to life after moving out of our home. They also expressed their sadness that Jon and I often did not get along, and I was constantly frustrated with him. We didn't want to admit it, but we realized that what they remembered and expressed was true. It wasn't until my husband got diagnosed with cancer that we could heal, forgive, and ask for forgiveness. And believe me, nothing makes you more powerful than the ability to forgive and seek forgiveness.

With all this being said, be sure to ask if you can do anything to mend the current situation. While not disregarding what happened, ask how your child might want to proceed with this and how you can do anything to help during this process of healing. You do not want to disconnect yourself from them as it may eventually result in ties being cut.

If we confess our sins, He is faithful and just and will forgive us our sins and purify us from all unrighteousness. — *1 John 1:9*

We are broken, and we need the grace of God to be a person who helps and encourages rather than hurts others.

Ten ways to let go of your adult children

Here are some additional guiding principles that we may have already discussed but can't be emphasized enough. "Letting go" is necessary and vital in allowing our adult kids to grow, mature, and be well-adjusted. But this will look different for every relationship, so trust your instincts as you go through the transition.

Birds of the sky know when it is time to let their babies leave their nests and spread their own wings. Humans tend to be a little slow in this regard. Our attachments are more than biology and go deeper than I'd suspect most animals can fathom.

According to the bible, the role of a parent involves the following job description: *receive, raise, and release.* As a parent of two daughters myself, I found it hard to let go of the reins that had been in place for 18 years.

As they slowly started spreading their own wings and finding their way in this weary world, the initial years saw me plagued with worry. But as they grew older and conflict resolution became a part of their daily life, seeing how they dealt with the people around them and resolved issues rather than just worry, feelings of pride started budding.

Not the ugly kind, but the beautiful one that slowly swelled in my heart when they recounted their day's happenings and goings-on. The casual confidence with which they soon learned to tackle the world with its many problems filled me with wonder and awe. God's creations truly are marvelous creatures!

Coming to terms with your adult child's own way of life is hard but most definitely not impossible. I've done it before, and I'm confident you will be able to do it too. Below are ten pointers that might aid you and make the 'letting go' process a little easier.

1. You start with baby steps. Literally!

The process of letting go starts with your toddlers' very first steps. In order to properly develop the ability to walk, your toddler needs to start by letting go of your hands and testing out their legs on their own. How will they know how to walk if you refuse to let go? As they grow older and school starts, you now have to let them go to school independently, where they can learn to socialize and make friends outside your family circle. Then comes high school with more freedom and eventually college. This is the stage where they become themselves as they get their first taste of real freedom. After college comes jobs, families, and so on and so forth. Letting go is a process, and if each step is dealt with swiftly, the next step becomes much easier.

2. Letting go doesn't mean you get to spend less time. It often means they will be willing to spend more time with you

You did what you could as a parent; now it's time to let them fly. I have come to find in my experience that allowing them to taste this freedom often makes them miss the comfort of home even more. So, if you were to let go of your child at the appropriate time, it is all the more likely that they will seek you out more often than if you keep clinging to them and not letting them go. Reverse psychology (of sorts) at its best.

3. God intended you to eventually let go

"Begin with the end in mind." These words were said by author Stephen Covey and are words I find highly pertinent to the subject matter at hand. What use is an arrow that is never used? Destiny dictates that if it stays in the comfort of the quiver, it will never acquire meaning or purpose. In all likelihood, it will rot. If you want to make your child a permanent resident of your home, ask yourself if you are doing this for yourself or for their well-being. Look at the big picture and the life God has in mind for them. While the comforts of home may be good for them, they will surely lose out on fulfilling God's plan for their lives in the long term.

4. Find a support group of mothers who are going through the same thing or have gone through the same thing

You cannot contest the wisdom of those who have lived and experienced. One mentor I found in my own life was my close friends in church and my parents. When I asked them if it got easier, they replied with an affirmative, and some even laughed and said life had so much more to offer to those willing to let go. Letting go is a gradual process where you slowly pull away and let them make their own decisions.

5. You are no longer their life coach and guru

Let go of the role you imposed on yourselves as they grew up. They've heard your advice, lessons, and wisdom. Now is the time they begin to put what they learned into practice, or not. Putting in your two cents too often will do more harm than good, as they may resist, even if it's good advice. If they come to you for advice, help, but do not overdo it! Better for them to want more of you than to run out of the room the second you stop talking. Letting go can be scary and stressful, so remember to pray and ask God for wisdom for you and your child.

6. You can no longer control them, and you need to come to terms with it

While control and a certain level of manipulation may have been necessary to control your child at a younger age, that intervention is no longer needed in their adult life. You need to let go of the reins and let them ride their own horse. Instead, you can take the role of a shoulder to lean on as a friend, cheerleader, and fan.

Keeping your tongue and expressions in check is crucial to not make your kid feel judged. Don't be quick to criticize, and avoid giving unwanted observations. Unless asked for, do not prompt extra information. You are you, and they are them. The sooner you realize that, the happier you will be.

7. Letting Go does NOT mean cutting off contact

Letting go is a gradual process that plays out over the years. While delaying it can have adverse consequences, rushing it might have even more serious repercussions. Once you begin letting go, this does not mean you dissolve all contact when they move out. You need to deal with it with tact and grace.

One cannot simply cut ties one day and expect their child to want to continue a cordial relationship. You cannot and must not absolve yourself of all responsibility for developing the relationship. The point is to let go, not cut off. Call, but not every day. Text, but not incessantly. There must be a balance.

8. You CANNOT and should NOT rush to rescue your child every time they fall or fail

Failure is a natural part of life. The sooner your kids learn and deal with this eventuality, the easier it will be for them to deal with it as they venture out into the world. One crucial part of letting go is NOT immediately rushing to your child's aid the second they fail or fall. While it may seem cold, this is the only way they can truly learn. This is not to say you do not help when they are in a grave situation. It just means to be prudent with what you react to.

As a parent, we are often hard-wired to be enablers. But this enabling cannot be why your child eventually cannot deal with the consequences of their own decisions. I know a couple who sent their daughter to a rehab center, not once or twice, but seven times. Each session cost them 20,000 to 30,000 a pop. While her parents clearly loved her, sometimes kids need to reach rock bottom in order to wake up and want to change. I realize this may be a hard pill to swallow, but necessary.

9. Both parents should be on the same page about letting go

If you and your spouse happen to have gone through a divorce, it becomes even more important to be up to date with the letting go program. Letting go is a group project involving both you and your child. You need to stand together in all circumstances when it comes to your child's growth and well-being.

10. Pass on the knowledge you have gained to other such parents letting go

This book is my attempt at sharing the wisdom I have learned over the years of motherhood and 'letting go' of my own daughters. It has been a great exercise in the reflexivity of my own actions and how I can improve, as our relationship is still ongoing and will surely be subject to many changes. Helping one another in areas of weakness is the best way to grow in your relations with your child, others, and God.

I just want to say that there are times when our kids make selfish, irresponsible, or dangerous choices that will directly or indirectly affect you as well. And there may be times when you need to intervene more aggressively, especially if drugs, depression, or violence are involved. Every situation is different, and every child is unique in their personality and maturity level. Seeking professional help from a trained therapist may be needed when the problems are too difficult and overwhelming.

Conclusion

Life is a process, and I believe that the saying 'you cannot teach an old dog new tricks' is highly flawed. We, as humans, will keep learning and growing. The process of learning to deal with your now adult children need not be riddled with potholes and bumps. While I cannot guarantee completely smooth sailing relations, if you keep the following key points in mind, the process of adjusting to your new reality and letting go can be much easier:

- Your new role will require you to adjust your expectations and your attitude. Balance is key in such situations and all circumstances. May you pray as never before, believing that God loves your child far more than you could.

- Listening and being a responsible parent is crucial to having good relations with your adult children. Do not take stances that are defensive and judgemental and not under any circumstances discount their experiences.

- Remember that letting go is crucial as it empowers your child to assume responsibility for his life. They learn how to depend upon God independently. Let His power in their life during their hardship be a testament to his living grace. Do not deprive them of the satisfaction that comes from making wise decisions.

CHAPTER THREE

DO STAY CONNECTED, DON'T BE QUICK TO SPEAK

When it comes to parenting adult children, perhaps one of the most difficult areas is communication. It's not uncommon for parents to say that they feel their children are distant, and many adult children say the same about their parents. So if you feel like you're no longer talking much to your child, or they aren't opening up to you anymore, then you're not alone. A lot of parents go through this situation.

But in such cases, how can you communicate better with your children? How do you develop a deeper, stronger bond with them even after they get older and move out to live their own lives? Well, in short, the best thing you can do to improve your relationship with them is to talk less and listen more but always stay engaged.

Stay Connected

When your son or daughter moves out (although some are living with their parents longer), connection is so important. I found that communication became more difficult as my girls were transitioning out of the house and being on their own. We went from seeing each other every day to only seeing them about once a week. As parents, we knew they needed their space and independence, but I missed them very much. I'm thankful that the phone was our lifeline, but they didn't share everything, and I had to accept that.

It used to be so easy. You'd tell or show your children how to act or what to do, and they'd do it. You taught them responsibility, told them to eat their veggies, and let them express themselves.

The same goes for parents of teenagers: There's certainly no lack of information out there for trying to deal with surly adolescents. But around the time your kids fly the coop, all this advice — all this communication about communication — suddenly disappears. They are off on their own, and it's a whole new ballgame. You're not living with them anymore, so how do you know when they need you? This might sound strange, but everyday chitchat is the answer.

Depending on your current relationship, work schedules, etc., you might talk to them every day, every few days, every week, or every few weeks. But no matter how often this communication happens — whether via phone, text, or in person — the crucial thing is to keep it regular. It shouldn't have to be a special occasion to have an honest conversation. If you're listening to and talking with your children, you might know something's wrong before they even tell you. And when you're communicating with them as equals, your advice won't seem overbearing or controlling.

Remember, too, that there will probably come a time when your roles reverse and your children are taking care of you, so keeping it open and friendly now will only make it better later. Don't be afraid to have those "big" conversations about money, illness, later-in-life care, and, yes, death. Trust us — doing it now will help you avoid a lot of problems and heartache.

Of course, there are going to be times when things aren't so easy and breezy.

Granted, some things just aren't easy to talk about — like when a child asks for a loan, has a new "significant other," wants to move back home, or is making bad decisions. But if you've been consistent with regular conversations, you should be able to weather any situation, no matter how dire it may seem. The more often you talk to your adult kids about everyday things, the easier it will be to talk about difficult things when the time comes. Chances are you'll notice when a problem starts brewing, and you'll know when to jump in and when to back off. Remember, it's about talking WITH your adult kids, not AT them. It might take every ounce of control to dispense advice, but try to wait until you're asked. AND avoid uttering phrases like "I told you so" and

"Someday, you'll see things my way." You'll just put your child on the defensive, and the conversation will quickly turn south. And while you do need to say what's on your mind, even if it's difficult, be careful how you say it. Be firm but supportive; it's better to get things out in the open than to let them fester.

Listening is Key

Listening is a skill, and a valuable one at that, one that will not only come in handy during parenting but in maintaining any relationship, whether it's with your partner, friends, or co-workers and acquaintances.

"Oh, but I am a great listener." Many parents think this way. I used to believe I was an excellent listener, and even more so when it came to my children. But if you're here, acknowledging that you're having a somewhat difficult time connecting to your children, then maybe the problem is that you're not listening well or not listening enough.

And it's not something you can consciously change overnight. People can't just wake up one day and remind themselves to be better listeners. No, it's a step-by-step process that includes some introspection, self-reflection, and a lot of hard work to let go of our protective and authoritative parenting mentality and slowly transition toward becoming more of a friend. So, when it comes to communicating with adult children, you need to accept two things firmly:

1. You should be open to listening, patient, and thoughtful before talking.

2. The process of being a better listener takes time and conscious mental reconditioning.

Even though we all know that listening is an important skill, it's just that. As parents, we sometimes fail to realize the importance of listening to our children. That is why the first step you must take is to understand the importance of listening when communicating with them.

My dear brothers, take note of this: Everyone should be quick to listen, slow to speak, and slow to become angry.   *— James 1:19*

Child vs. Adult

When your children were kids, you were their caregivers. Providing for them, protecting them, teaching them, and showing the world to them – you had to do all these things. And as children, they had very few meaningful things to say to you. They were like an empty glass, filling themselves up by observing and learning. Like any adult, your child now has their thoughts, beliefs, perceptions, and opinions. They don't need you to act like a strict teacher anymore, as they are learning to make their own decisions and discern between right and wrong. Even if they haven't become as mature and responsible as adults should be, it's already past the stage to teach them life skills. Now is the time to be their friend and role model, a kind and understanding figure.

You can still be of great importance in their lives, helping and guiding them at every stage, but you can't do it the same way you used to when they were, let's say, in their early teens. You must first accept that as an adult, they should and will make their own decisions. Your role is to help them make their life decisions in the best way possible, but through wise guidance, not authoritative command.

But for you to support them in their lives, you have to know what they are thinking, feeling, and doing. Sometimes, your child may reach out and try to share something that's bothering them. At other times, you will have to be the one to initiate contact and ask them how they are doing. Moments like these are when you should listen attentively to your children. Only then will you understand how you can help them and, most importantly, encourage them to make the right decisions.

That means communication with adult children becomes two-way. You need to listen to them now because they are no longer empty cups, and you have to understand what is filled in their cups before you can give them advice or suggestions.

Throughout their childhood, they have spent many years listening to you and how you guided them physically, mentally, emotionally, and socially. It's only fair for the roles to reverse now and for you to be the one to listen to them.

Why is it challenging for parents to listen more often to adult children?

You probably know this, but before Galileo, people spent years and years believing that it was the sun that revolved around the earth. So when Galileo used his telescope and suggested that the Earth revolved around the sun and not the other way, he was accused of heresy and put on trial.

You may wonder what this has to do with parenting. I am trying to point out that when people spend a long time firmly believing in something, it becomes incredibly difficult to change that way of thinking, especially when someone challenges those beliefs. As parents, we spend a good 18 years nurturing our children, being their guide and teacher, and holding a position of authority over them. But when they grow into adults, you cannot treat them the same way. You can't scold, reprimand, or command.

And this is something a lot of parents struggle with – to change their perspective towards their children and their approach towards dealing with them. After seeing them as innocent kids and naive teenagers for almost two decades, it's very hard to come to terms with the fact that they are a person of their own now.

For some parents, it's also an issue of coming to terms with the fact that they have to let their children go, something I talked about in the previous chapter as well. But for every parent, it can be different things that they need to let go of, such as:

- Some parents struggle with physically letting go of their children when they decide to leave and find their own place.

- For many parents, the challenge is also to let go of their child emotionally, especially for those who have been deeply attached to their children from a young age.

- Sometimes, the issue may be letting go of your authority, where you may find it hard to accept that you are no longer the one who makes their decisions anymore.

- Perhaps the biggest challenge is to let go of your children when they're doing something that goes against your own wishes or beliefs, for example, if your child chooses to pursue a different religion someday. They have the right to make their life choices, but when it's something you may not approve of, it will obviously be a very difficult pill to swallow.

To sum things up, there are two reasons why parents find it hard actually to listen to their adult Kids:

1. After serving as a teacher, caregiver, provider, and authority figure for so many years, it's difficult to break away from that role and see our children as capable adults who need their parents to become loving and caring friends, not vigilant guardians.

2. Given the immense bond and connection with our children, it's always going to be challenging and tough to let go of them, even more so when you two have different beliefs and opinions.

The Benefits of Listening to Your Children

Here are some compelling reasons parents need to spend more time listening to their children and the benefits it will have in your relationship:

1. You understand your child's beliefs and their view of the world. This will give you a better insight into their their way of thinking and decision making.

2. When you get to know the adult selves of your children at a deeper level, you're in a better position to realize their strengths and identify where they are struggling in life. Are they unprepared for the responsibilities of adulthood? Are they lacking self-discipline? Or perhaps they are struggling with financial responsibilities now that they have to take care of their own income and expenses.

3. And once you understand their problems and the ins and outs of their lives, you'll be able to give them better advice and suggestions.

4. Even if your child isn't necessarily looking for advice, simply listening to what they are going through will cement your position in their lives as a reliable person to share their joys and sorrows with. They will know that if they ever need to vent after a bad day at work or express excitement after a long-awaited promotion, they can always share those moments with you before anyone else.

When you listen more and talk less, your children will start to see you as a friend, guide, and someone they can constantly rely on whenever they need advice, suggestions, or just an extra set of ears to hear their thoughts or problems. Over time, they will value your role and make you an important part of their lives.

But if we look at it from the other end, there are many ways in which your relationship can weaken if you don't listen to them. The tricky thing is that no parent 'chooses' not to listen to their children. We don't shut down our ears or intentionally talk over them when they say something. But what really happens is that we see things from our perspective and try to act like the same parent figure we were when they were kids or teens.

Here's an example. Let's say your son or daughter calls to tell you they are considering quitting their current, well-paying job. Maybe it's not a position they are happy with, and the work culture is unhealthy. But while they explain their thoughts, our minds can drift towards other things, thanks to our "parental instincts." We may start to worry about their financial security, if they have a backup plan, if they have another job in sight, or if they need some financial support until they get another job.

All these are important things, no doubt. But if you bring these issues out right away in the conversation, you're cutting them off, even though you intend to help them. This is just one example of how parents unintentionally fail to listen to their kids. There will be many instances where we try to do our best for our children, but we take a hasty approach and step in too soon.

Do this too often, and your child may feel distant. Sometimes, you may not even realize they feel that way. They could have a busy work life, so you think that is why they don't call very often or don't talk too long when you call them, but you may be unaware that they are hesitant to open up to you. Moments like these can quickly build up and strain your connection with your children.

So, on the one hand, taking the time to listen to your children carefully enables you to act as a strong support in their lives and a close friend. On the other hand, if you're not putting in the time and effort to listen to them actively, it could create communication barriers in your relationship in the long term.

Be completely humble and gentle; be patient, bearing with one another in love.
                                            — Ephesians 4:2

Eight Ways for Parents of Adult Children to Become Better Listeners

Don't be overly concerned if you already feel that your child is growing a little distant. Questioning ourselves if we've been poor listeners as parents are unpleasant, but it's not the be-all and end-all of things. It's never too late to make things right and take conscious steps toward becoming a better parent by being a better listener.

It won't be easy because there are no instructions or a manual that tells you how to be an active and patient listener. What it really takes is a series of small steps – in your mindset, your approach, and your actions. Here are ten effective tips for all parents to improve how they communicate with their children by listening more and talking less.

1. Change your parenting approach

In the previous chapter, I talked about shifting parenting roles and changing how we deal with our children. You can't force yourself to be a better listener. First, you must adjust to a new parenting approach where you have completely accepted that you are no longer the captain of their ship. You now need to let them take control of the ship and be by their side as a trusted guide and advisor.

Mentally prepare yourself to settle into this new role slowly.

2. Embrace gradual transition

The transition from late teens to adulthood is quite subtle, but that is when your child experiences key personality development. The teen years are the most formative period of your child's life. That is when they begin to develop their beliefs, morals, and ambitions. So naturally, this is the phase where parents tend to be most active, discussing key decisions for their children's future, working hard to provide for their education and development financially, and preparing them to one day look after themselves.

But those years eventually pass by, and before you know it, your children have completed college, secured a job, and are moving out. Throughout all those years, you must embrace a gradual transition in dealing with them. By the time they enter adulthood, they need to be responsible and take control of their own life. This acceptance will put you in the right mindset needed to become a better listener.

3. Shift from teacher to mentor

One of the parents' biggest responsibilities is raising their child to become a responsible person. Home is the first school for children, and parents are the first teachers. From a tender age, we teach our children about proper etiquette, morals, social behaviors, learning, acquiring skills, and many other things to help them lead a good life.

During these early years, our role as a teacher means that we do most of the talking. We instruct them, praise them, sometimes reprimand them, and always encourage them. But after adulthood, we need to put away the role of teacher and step into the shoes of a mentor.

Do you know what the most important characteristics of a mentor are? They don't have personal expectations. Their role is to effectively guide others in achieving their goals and ambitions. So when you act as a mentor to your child, your responsibility is to help them build the life 'they' want, and not the life 'you want for them.' By doing so, you will put the focus on what your child wants to make of their life, and it will make you more receptive towards listening to their desires, career plans, and other important decisions.

I remember making this shift from teacher to mentor when my oldest daughter was experiencing some real heartbreaks during her 20s and early 30s. While her sister was married with two children, Karina desperately wanted a husband and children as well. Poor choices, break ups, and discouragement seemed never-ending, and as her mom, I empathized with her frustrations. Sometimes she would reach out to me for advice, but other times, she was distant, tight-lipped, and didn't want to share. I had to learn not to pry or ask too many questions if she was upset. As I stepped back and let her approach me when she needed to, our relationship improved. I began accepting my role as a mentor and not a teacher. Our kids will experience hurt and disappointment, but it is necessary for growth and maturity. I couldn't choose a mate for Karina, but God did when the time was right.

4. Reserve judgment and advice

As adults, your child has to make their own decisions and handle the consequences of their actions. It's the learning process in life that we all go through. At this time, the best parents can do is provide them with moral and mental support to make the right choices and be responsible.

But in doing so, we must be wary of passing judgment. Avoid getting upset over something they did or saying things like "I told you so" or "You should have listened to me." It's normal for you to get upset, but expressing disappointment or agitation will not make your child feel any better.

Meeting their boyfriend, girlfriend, or fiance for the first time should be exciting, but oftentimes it's not. You wonder how these two ever got together. Their choice in a partner is less than desirable, but it's important to reserve judgment. Over time, their true colors emerge, bringing clarity about the relationship. Tread lightly when expressing concern, and if a breakup or divorce occurs, be there with love and encouragement.

Even if you're not upset but want to offer healthy advice, don't dish it out unless asked. There's nothing wrong with offering advice as a parent, but first, you must see the complete picture. Encourage them to open up and share their problems with you. Once they have poured out their hearts to you, ask them if they want advice. Sometimes, they may only need someone to talk to and feel better.

The best you can do is always be verbal about the fact that you are always there to offer them help in any way you can. If they can share things with you without the fear of being judged, they will be comfortable coming to you for advice on their own when they need it.

5. Are you a good listener? Why not find it out?

Some people are naturally calm, reserved, and patient listeners. Some are energetic, filled with ideas and enthusiasm, and often do more talking. It's not you but the people you interact with who can tell how good of a listener you are. Be more active and aware in your conversations with everyone, not just your children.

You are a good listener if:

- Your child comes up to you on their own to share their problems

- People you talk to are often interested and engaged in the conversation

- You find yourself asking more questions during the conversation

So be more attentive to these cues when talking to your children and other people around you, like family and co-workers. Also, remember that hearing and listening aren't the same thing. The difference is that listening requires attention. Not just your ears but also your mind and focus need to be on the speaker. Try to be aware if your mind tends to drift off to your own thoughts when conversing with people.

6. Initiate conversations

When your children begin their journey to adulthood, they face many new aspects of life, and it can be both an exciting and overwhelming experience. In the rush of it all, it's not uncommon for them to get too occupied in their own lives. During such times, it's your responsibility to call or text them occasionally just to catch up and ask them what they have been to lately. At the same time, you have to be careful not to come across as intrusive, so set some limits and try to initiate conversations now and then.

You can also make time for occasional family dinners, as it is a perfect setup for casual conversation. If you want to hear how your child is settling into their new apartment, new job, or new relationship, or if there's something important to discuss, such as moving to another city, state, or country, it's a great idea to discuss these things one on one. If you can set up a schedule for a parent-children dinner night, let's say once a month or so, it will be a nice occasion to bring all these important topics on the table along with the good food.

It will make room for healthy conversations and allow you to sit and listen to your children and be a part of their life experiences.

7. Accept differences in opinion

Again, one of the hardest aspects of parenting adult children is that there will be differences in opinions and beliefs. The tricky part is that you must be very careful and discerning in your actions. Sometimes, it can be clear that your child is about to make a wrong decision. Even then, you can't step in and command them to act otherwise. Like any adult, you need to reason with them and make them realize they are taking the wrong step.

Other times, it's not so black and white, and you may disagree on things without either being right or wrong. For example, your child may be eager to start their own business, but you may see it as a risky step and would rather prefer they stay put at their job. There's nothing wrong with both perspectives, but if they want to start a business, you could support them instead of opposing them.

Try to be open to their ideas and approach when there are contrasting views. It will make you a better listener and allow you to embrace a new point of view from the eyes of your children.

8. Become a friend

Lastly, the best advice I can give all parents – once your children are adults, do whatever you can to become a friend. It's the best role you can play in their lives. Let me tell you why.

Think about all your friends, every single friend you have made in your life so far. Then think how many of them are your closest friends, people you truly care for and respect. There have been frequent surveys to measure how many friends a person has on average. And there have been varying figures, but it's always a small number, less than ten.

We meet countless people and carefully choose only a few to be our closest friends. It shows that friendship is valuable, and we only share it with selected people. So it only makes sense to share a level of friendship with your child. Friends are also among the first people we go to when we want to share something. If your child begins to see you as a friend, they will enjoy communicating with you and value your advice and opinions. Don't forget texting is fine for short, informal communication but should not be the "modus operandi" of choice. Talking things out over the phone or in person is much more effective, and words don't get "lost in translation."

Actions Speak Louder than Words

Yes, how we communicate makes a huge difference, but communicating through our actions is equally as important. We will never stop being their parents, and we can express love in so many tangible ways. What could we do for our adult kids just to let them know that we care, especially if there's tension, hurt, or unresolved issues? Inviting them to lunch or a movie, dropping off a few groceries, sending a plant or card in the mail, texting them a special song or a memorable photo, or babysitting the grandkids, are just a few ideas. Showing love with tangible actions says, "I care about you and our relationship." Remember the saying by Benjamin Franklin: "Well done is better than well said."

Conclusion

Keeping open, honest communication is key to preserving a healthy relationship with your adult kids. Listening to them and allowing them to express their feelings without reacting will help to diffuse a potential argument.

As an adult, your child may have the right and freedom to make their own decisions, but that doesn't mean your role as a parent ends here. You only need to adapt to a new approach when parenting adult children, requiring you to make changes within yourself first. And one such important change is to start listening more and talking less.

Once your children set out to lead independent lives, you will have to consciously try to catch up with them and know them better. That's why it's important to encourage children to speak up to you and for you to be patient and listen to them before you decide on what you should say or do. Acts of love and kindness also go a long way to help bridge those gaps when things get messy.

CHAPTER FOUR

DO HELP, DON'T ENABLE

As parents, we always want the best for our children. Our love and concern for them stay strong even when they grow up and become adults. And this love towards our children drives us to provide them with all they need to live a happy, successful life.

However, your good intentions to care for and support your adult children can often go overboard, and you may unknowingly or unintentionally enable them. The term 'enable' usually has a positive tone and meaning. To enable means to make it easier for something to happen. But in parenting, the meaning is quite the opposite.

Enabling your adult children means that you don't let them experience the regular hardships of life and naturally occurring unpleasant situations. There are many ways you could be enabling your children, such as:

- Fixing their problems

- Saving them from the consequences of their wrong actions
- Financially supporting them even after adulthood
- Making decisions on their behalf

In general, if you're making your children's lives too easy by doing things they should be handling themselves, 'you're enabling' them. And it can have many detrimental effects on your child and their development. Furthermore, reinforcing such enabling behaviors can also take a toll on you long-term and ruin your relationship with your children.

The main issue is parents don't usually enable their adult children intentionally. From your point of view, you'll feel like you're supporting and helping them. But due to your love and perhaps your parental instincts to some extent, your efforts to help them may encourage them to be increasingly dependent on you.

So, in this chapter, we'll dive deeper into this practice of subconsciously or unknowingly enabling adult children. We'll discuss how and why parents may be doing it without being aware of its serious negative effects. Going through this chapter, at one point, some of you may realize that you have been inadvertently enabling your children. Don't worry because awareness and acceptance are the first steps toward rectification. And I have also explained a highly effective 3-step process for parents to break out of this harmful practice while transitioning towards a healthier relationship where you become an important support system for your adult child without sheltering them or making them reliant.

What are the negative effects of enabling?

Before everything else, you really need to understand how dangerous and harmful it can be to enable adult children. Of course, it may not always be a big deal, but the longer you continue sheltering them from unpleasant situations, the more serious problems it will create for everyone.

When you actively enable your children, it has a ripple effect that influences you and your child in many ways. Overall, its negative effects can be explained in three categories:

How it affects your child

- It makes them dependent. When you protect them from tough situations and come to their rescue repeatedly, they'll depend on you for most things. It's a part of human nature that we always prefer the easiest option. By enabling your child, you're making their life easier, and that subconsciously reinforces a mindset that anytime things go south for them, you'll be there to take care of things.

- Children dependent on their parents also lack important qualities such as confidence and mental and emotional strength. Independence and responsibilities are a major part of every person's personality development. If you don't let your children experience their own freedom and decision-making, they'll only be 'adults' by age but still 'children' in terms of life experience.

- It hinders their transition to adulthood, as they will be unprepared for responsibilities. If you keep making decisions for them, solving all their problems, and protecting them from life's struggles, they will never learn important life lessons. They won't realize what it's like to face the consequences of one's actions, make tough decisions, and become stronger and more responsible by going through hardships. The problems and struggles we face play a huge role in bringing maturity and a sense of responsibility to us. But when you enable children, you prevent them from obtaining the maturity that comes from facing life challenges and hurdles.

- You won't live forever; one day, you'll have to leave the world and your children. When parents enable their children for too long, they never learn to fend for themselves financially, mentally, or emotionally. As the parents eventually pass away, such children are suddenly left helpless and defenseless. Teaching our children how to live their lives responsibly and successfully is an important part of parenting, but children who have been enabled and sheltered by their parents never learn such things. So, when you inevitably pass away one day, your children will suddenly realize the harsh reality that they are incapable of taking care of themselves without you.

- The worst part of enabling adult children is that they never learn to take responsibility for their actions, especially their wrongdoings. If you're saving and protecting them every time, they stop fearing the repercussions of their transgressions. And that might only encourage them to daringly commit more offenses, ultimately ending down the wrong path in life.

You can shield them from troubles all you want, but you can't save them from the judgment of the Lord. If you don't let them learn from hardships, difficult responsibilities, and, most importantly, the consequences of wrong actions, one day, it will all catch up with them. In fact, they might even lose the fear of God and the ability to discern between right and wrong.

For he who does wrong will receive the consequences of the wrong which he has done, and that without partiality. — Colossians 3:25

How it affects you as a parent

When our decisions and actions lead to unpleasant circumstances, we must face them ourselves as adults. If you keep making decisions for your children even though they are adults, you will be held responsible for their lives. The onus will always be on you to justify the things your children do, both good and bad. You will unnecessarily add extra burden on your life when you keep caring for adult children. At first, enablement always starts with good intentions –

your love for them and desire to keep them happy. Over time, it can become a burden you put upon yourself that you can't escape easily either.

How it affects your parent-child relationship

The worst part of enabling adult children is that it initially seems very healthy. Your child will probably be happy and ecstatic to know that whenever they need something, they can just ask you for it. You'll come to their rescue immediately whenever they are in trouble. Whenever they need to get some difficult work done, they can just ask you to do it on their behalf.

At first, they'll most likely express much love and gratitude for such favors. And seeing them in good spirits will make you happy as well. You might even feel like you're playing your part as a loving parent by caring for them in every aspect. But these are all temporary joys, and like it or not, such a seemingly beautiful relationship will take a huge toll sooner or later.

The love you get from your children isn't really for you, but for the favors they get from you. If you can't help them at any point, that love will vanish quickly. When parents enable children, their relationship will not be based on unconditional love but on a pretentious foundation of receiving favors.

Then there's another equally worrisome scenario. At first, your child may enjoy the privilege of relying on you for everything, but obviously, you can't do anything and everything for them. So, there will come a time when they'll have to face challenges no matter how hard you try to shelter them. And when that time comes, they will suddenly come to terms with the fact that they are incapable of living independently because you have made them that way. Someday, they will probably realize on their own that the years you spent enabling them have made them severely unprepared for the harsh realities of life. They will have failed to 'grow up' in the true sense, and they may resent you for it.

Sometimes, the relationship can turn sour on your end as well. If you spend a lot of time enabling your children, they will come to expect the same. Initially, everything you do for them is out of your own choice, but when it becomes routine, you'll feel obliged to continue taking care of them. Eventually, your children will start to feel like a burden, and you may resent them instead.

So there are many ways your parent-child relationship can deteriorate if you keep enabling them for a long time.

Even the Lord makes it clear that every person has to fulfill their own responsibilities and carry their own cross.

Each one must examine his own work, and then he will have reason to boast with regard to himself alone, and not with regard to someone else; 5 for each will bear his own load. One who is being instructed in the word should share all good things with his instructor. Make no mistake: God is not mocked, for a person will reap only what he sows. — *Galatians 6: 4-7*

When you truly acknowledge the gravity and seriousness of this practice of enabling children, it becomes clear that there is nothing good and fruitful about it in the long term. But what should you do then? How can you make sure that you don't enable your adult children? First and foremost, are you even aware if you've been enabling them?

Let us now go through different ways of identifying enabling behaviors and stopping them altogether so that your children can learn, grow, and flourish by experiencing both the highs and lows of life.

How Do Parents Enable Children?

The most common way that parents enable adult children is through financial support. This can include things like paying the rent for your adult child, buying them a car, allowing them to stay with you or move back home, continually giving them money, purchasing a home for a child, and similar behaviors. Helping your child at some points in life when they have fallen on hard times may be necessary. Still, continual financial support is not healthy for adult children or parents.

Emotional support can also be seen as enabling. Although parents should offer unconditional love for their children, emotional dependence is a far cry from general parental support; parents who consistently come to their children's emotional rescue to boost self-esteem are engaging in an emotionally enabling relationship. Although parents can and should encourage their children, regularly telling a child, "They're just jealous..." or "You deserve it..." or "You're too good for them..." and other phrases are common with emotionally-enabling parents. They can encourage problematic behavior.

Another way that parents could be enabling grown children is by allowing inappropriate communication and even encouraging it. Adult children who are rude, disrespectful, and perpetually critical of parents are being enabled in poor communication and unhealthy communicative behavior. Although parents and children are certain to have disagreements, and you are certainly within reason to express disappointment, frustration, or disagreement with a parent, consistently shouting, abusing, or otherwise inappropriately communicating with a parent is not behavior that can be allowed or encouraged. Many parents resign themselves to this manner of speech, but allowing adult children to engage in unhealthy communication encourages them to use that type of communication with others.

I wish my husband and I had realized the harm we were doing by enabling our daughters. And it started way before they were adults. I shared earlier about the negative behaviors we brought into our marriage and the mistakes we made as parents. We weren't on the same page when it came to finances and budgeting. And we definitely didn't agree on much when it came to raising the girls. Jon loved them but had a hard time expressing it, so spending money on them was what he did.

Me: "Jon, are you taking the girls shopping again?"

Jon: "Don't worry about it."

Me: "Well, they don't need jeans from stores at the mall. They are way too expensive!"

Jon: "Don't worry about it."

Me: "And you shouldn't give them money any time they ask for it."

Jon: "Don't worry about it."

These were conversations that never got resolved, and the spending cycle continued. Most of our heated discussions had to do with spending money on the girls. He also bought them each a car after graduating high school. Yes, they worked and continued their education, but teaching them the discipline of saving wasn't something we were very good at. Those early adulthood years were stressful, frustrating, and challenging for all of us. The transition out of the house to being on their own was like trying to find their way out of a dark room. There was no direction or clear expectations for them or us as parents.

Shawna was married with a baby at 21, and both she and her new husband were fairly responsible and financially independent. Karina, on the other hand, continued to receive some help with rent and car payments until she was married many years later. She even moved back home for a few months to save money. But she also learned valuable lessons along the way by budgeting and living within her means.

Looking back, things could have gotten much worse as Jon and I both enabled our daughters. He, the spender, and me, the doer. I did so many things for them that they could and should have done for themselves, which is the definition of enabling. In spite of our shortcomings, I'm proud of whom they have become.

How to stop enabling and start helping your children

When your child enters adulthood, you must guide them toward independence. So you have to be very careful in your approach not to unknowingly encourage any type of enabling behaviors. It can seem a bit confusing, but there's a simple 3-step process you can follow to shift your parenting approach from "enabling" to "helping" so that instead of sheltering them from all bad things, you allow them to become strong enough to fight their own battles and make their own decisions.

Step 1: Awareness

The first step is to understand the differences between helping and enabling so that you can be clear about whether or not you are enabling them without realizing it.

Step 2: Preparation

If you realize that you've been enabling your child, you can't just stop it immediately. You've made them dependent on you, so you can't just leave them to their own devices all of a sudden. That's setting them up for failure. You need to prepare and plan small steps to make long-lasting changes carefully.

Step 3: Gradual transition

69

The change has to be gradual so that your adult child can slowly start to handle their own life. Even you need time to accept that you cannot and should not do everything for them, that they also need to experience the difficult moments and learn from them. So you need to make certain small changes over time to let go of your child one step at a time, let them experience freedom, fend for themselves, and clean up their own mess.

Now let us understand each of these steps in detail.

Step 1: Awareness – Knowing the difference between helping and enabling

The difference between helping, empowering, and enabling is not always clear, so it can get tricky to identify enabling behaviors in some situations. Your love and emotions will also make it difficult for you to determine whether what you do for them counts as helping or enabling. Because in your heart, you'll feel like you're only doing what's good for them, or to word it correctly, what 'you think' is good for them.

To help your adult child means to show them how they can fend for themselves, face their own challenges, and become independent. Helping them means empowering them. It could be in the form of advice, encouragement, instructions, or any form of direct or indirect support that guides them while still allowing them to make the final decision and take the necessary actions with their own hands.

To enable your adult child means removing them from tough and negative situations that they should otherwise be facing naturally. Can you imagine a life without problems? Did you live a life where you didn't have to worry about anything? Such a life doesn't exist for anyone.

Everyone has their fair share of life problems, which serve as lessons. They make us wiser and stronger. So it's only reasonable that your children should go through the same phase and experience their share of problems and challenges. But when you enable them, you end up sheltering them from all such unpleasant instances in life.

Some examples to demonstrate the difference between helping and enabling:

Case 1: Your child wants to buy a car, and you can afford it.

Enabling: You buy them a car. With your best intentions, of course, you tell them they need to be responsible and take care of the vehicle. But just because you can afford it without any problem, you buy it for them right away.

Helping: You help them to earn for the car. Or, you could pay for some of it but still encourage them to manage the rest of the money. You can help them secure a job. If they're already working, you can help them save some cash. You can even assist them in finding a reasonably priced vehicle that fits within their budget.

Key Takeaway: This example relates to all situations where your child "wants" something. They might not be in trouble or struggling with making crucial decisions, but they simply want something.

If you're readily providing them with what they want just because you want to make them happy, that's enabling. If you can afford those things, it may seem trivial to you. But they won't learn the struggles of earning what they want, nor will they experience the joy of accomplishment. Sure, getting a car or a home from your parents might feel good, but earning your first car or buying your first home is a much more satisfying feeling, isn't it?

If you want to help in such situations, first analyze whether what they want is necessary for them. If it is, help them figure out a way to make their own money, work hard, and save up. Let them learn the lesson that we all need to earn what we desire and require.

Case 2: Your child is underperforming at work and is under fire by their boss.

Enabling: You see your child is unhappy at their job and tell them to quit if they aren't enjoying the work. You might agree to offer financial support for as long as it takes until they get a new job. Or perhaps you'll pull some strings with people you know to secure them another opportunity.

Helping: You try to figure out why they are underperforming. Is it due to their own fault, such as laziness and demotivation to work? Or is it the company's fault, due to poor work ethics or excess work pressure?

If it's their fault, you must let them realize that nothing comes without hard work. Encourage them to become more active and responsible in the office. Let them face the music if they don't heed your advice. Maybe they'll get fired, and when they do, you need to toughen up and tell them that their own actions have caused this. Don't spoil them by providing them with money. You can offer them some support for a month or maybe two. But after that, if they still don't find a new job and change their sluggish ways, you have to step back and let them struggle financially so that they can learn the lesson.

And if it's the company that is putting unfair pressure on your child, that is when you can help them quit and guide them in finding a better work environment.

Key Takeaway: This case basically represents all scenarios where your child is in some sort of trouble or difficulty.

Enabling is when you instantly come to their rescue without analyzing the situation. Your only priority will be to get them away from trouble and get them back to a comfortable spot as quickly as possible.

Helping is when you first determine if the trouble or difficulty is because of your child's actions or other external factors and then offer them a proper way to solve it. Even then, you let them carry out the solution on their own. You also ensure that they learn from the hardships and become wiser to avoid similar predicaments in the future. In worse cases, if they land in trouble but still don't try to correct their ways, the best help you can offer them is to just sit back and let them suffer the ill consequences of their mistakes. Sometimes, life itself is the best teacher.

Case 3: Your child is in jail and wants you to bail him out.

Enabling: You bail them out. Sure, you may have a strict word with them and reprimand them for getting on the wrong side of the law. But if you're bailing them out immediately, it might indirectly encourage them to repeat the misdemeanor or offense, thinking you'll come to their rescue anyway.

Helping: If they are behind bars, they've done something wrong. You should first analyze the gravity of their actions.

Is it a minor misdemeanor or felony? Then you may consider bailing them out with a warning that if they repeat it, they better not call you for help again.

But what if it's a serious crime? Then the right thing to do is let them face their sentence in jail and undergo reformation. At least the time in jail can turn them into a better person and teach them not to get on the wrong side of the law again.

Key Takeaway: Sure, this example might seem a bit extreme, but you can see it as a representation of all general cases where your child has done something wrong and landed in serious trouble. In such cases, you should refrain from rescuing them or solving their problems. Facing the consequence of serious mistakes is a part of the learning process in life. Don't take that away from them. It can be hard to see your child go through extremely hard times, but if they've made big mistakes to deserve such a fate, then best to let them bear the brunt. Saving them in such cases will only encourage them to repeat the same offenses without fear, punishment, or suffering. And one day, their actions will all build up to lead to a much bigger and worse consequence that can even ruin their whole life.

To sum things up briefly, the best way to understand the difference between enabling and helping is to consider the example of a teacher. Teachers provide students with the knowledge, information, and know-how to solve problems, but the students must do the solution. That's how you help and empower them. If the teacher comes to class and writes all the solutions on the board so students can copy them down, that's the equivalent of enabling your children as a parent.

Step 2: Preparation – Making small initial changes

Once you acknowledge that you've been unwittingly enabling your adult children, it's time to make some changes. Even if you aren't already doing so, taking precautions in advance is still advisable. Maybe your child is still in their teens but entering adulthood very soon. In that case, too, you can benefit by practicing small changes and habits early on.

Whatever the case, when you enter this preparation phase, here are a few things you need to focus on to stop yourself from enabling your adult children.

Change starts with yourself

Change your own mindset and approach. Realize that you are not in charge of your adult children anymore. Shift your parenting role by becoming a friend, confidant, and trusted advisor. Accept that you are not a provider and caregiver now. All these are things that we have discussed in earlier chapters, so you can revise them once again.

Grow a thick skin and start practicing 'tough' love

You need to mentally and emotionally brace yourself to bear seeing your children in trouble and despair without intervening or coming to their rescue. Whether it's something as simple as an argument with their friend or partner or serious issues such as running out of money to pay bills and put food on the table, you need to allow your child to face difficulties in life. If it hurts you to see them in any discomfort or distress, condition your mind and your heart from today itself so that you can practice tough love and let them suffer, as long as there is a lesson to be learned from it.

Talk to them about the concept of enabling

As adults, your children are also capable of understanding the negative effects of enabling. They, too, can comprehend that we all have to face hardships, which only make us stronger in life. So be open to your children about these things. Make it clear to them that they will have to take care of many things on their own now. Let them process that they are now the captain of their own ship. These things can be discussed even before your child hits adulthood so that they can be aware and prepare themselves for the responsibilities of adult life.

Of course, just because you want them to take care of themselves doesn't mean you are no longer available to help them. Let them know they can always come to you for help, but they shouldn't expect you to clean up their mess or fix their problems.

Step 3: Gradual Transition – Slow but Important Steps to Stop Enabling

When it comes to taking actionable steps to stop enabling behaviors, you need to be slow and gradual. Just because hardships make us stronger doesn't mean you throw everything at your child at once. The shift from teen to adult is a huge leap, and it takes time for people to get accustomed to such a big change. You can't just send them on their own way as soon as they turn 18 and let them take care of their own lives from day one, right?

And what about parents who already have adult children? What about parents who have just realized that they have actually enabled their adult children in many ways for quite some time now? In such cases, it is even more important to make very slow and subtle changes, so they don't feel like you've suddenly abandoned them.

So here are 5 simple tips you can implement slowly, one at a time.

Ground rules and boundaries

First things first, set clear boundaries and ground rules when it comes to the relationship between you and your adult child. When is it okay for them to ask you for money? In what areas are you willing to help them out, and what are the things you expect them to do on their own?

One great example is that if your child asks to stay at your place longer, even after turning 18, but you also want them to start learning financial responsibility, you can agree that they'll have to find some work and pay you a small amount as rent. But you also need to clarify that it's not because you want money from them, but more so to help them become financially independent when they get their own place someday.

So a good way to start helping your adult children is by agreeing upon some boundaries and rules that can benefit both of you.

Stop giving excessive financial support

One of the most prominent cases of enabling adult children is by providing them with consistent financial support. It may not seem like a big deal if you're earning a decent income. And it can also be hard to watch your child struggle with their bills when you have enough money to help them out. But that is just a short-term solution, and the only proper solution is for your child to earn for themselves in the long term. If they are in financial difficulty, focus more on helping them learn to earn and save instead of handing them out money every time they need it.

Encouragement, motivation, positive affirmations

Sometimes, all it takes for parents to empower their children is to just express their belief and trust in them. In tough times, encourage them to fight through. Remind them of their strengths and talents. Motivate them, and do it out loud. Tell them that you are confident in their abilities and that the hardships will pass as long as they hold their ground. Our children often don't want to be spoon-fed by us and handle their problems on their own. Instead, they might need a little boost of confidence and encouragement.

Be a friend and emotional support

In some situations, maybe your children aren't expecting advice, motivation, or direct help but just want someone they can pour their hearts out to. And who is closer to them than their own parents? So at times, you just need to be their friend, listen to their problems, give them a shoulder to rest their weary heads on, and serve as a constant emotional support.

Let them solve their own problems

The one thing you should avoid at all costs is fixing your child's problems. Even if they call out to you for help, just offer them useful advice and show them the right way. But let them take the necessary action with their own hands. Problem-solving is one of the most crucial skills in life, and it is learned only through life experience. No matter how big of a problem your child is facing, be their support and guide but make sure that they are the ones to put in the work and effort in the end.

Here's an open letter to parents who financially support adult kids, written by author and speaker, Peter Dunn in *USA Today (Nov. 2016)*:

> I write to you not from a place of judgment, but instead, I address you based on an immense body of work that has brought me great clarity. The financial support you are offering your adult children is toxic. You are hurting them, you are hurting yourself, and until you realize it's not money that they need, everyone involved will feel the pain.
>
> Think back to when you taught your child to ride her bicycle without training wheels. Who was more scared? The idea of letting go of a toddler rocketing across concrete with little protection is terrifying. If you let go, she will fall — she will bleed. If you don't, she will never learn to ride the most elementary transportation device since the invention of feet. Once you let go, and she falls and bleeds, she will quickly learn that balance and control equal the absence of pain. At that moment, everyone moves on with their life.
>
> Assuming your now twenty- or thirty-something can ride their bike without training wheels, what was the primary element in their initial bike-riding achievement? It was your willingness to remove yourself from the situation, with the disturbing knowledge your absence would result in pain.
>
> If you are still supporting your adult child, your absence will lead to their success — not your financial support. You have to remove yourself from the situation. As you look at your adult child's life, what is missing? Your child lacks skills in budgeting, resourcefulness, and, potentially, restraint.
>
> To be fair, if your child's problems stem from student loans, then their lack of independence actually makes

sense. However, you must be willing to acknowledge the amount of debt our children hold is directly correlated to our willingness and ability to pre-fund those college expenses, as well as our willingness to encourage our children to blindly accumulate hundreds of thousands of dollars of debt, with absolutely no plan to pay it off.

There's a giant chasm that exists between not being able to pre-fund an education and encouraging your children to pursue what their 18-year-old minds think is an ideal education. That gap can be bridged with uncomfortable conversations and restraint. Ignoring the chasm will result in everyone involved falling in.

In most cases that I've seen of parents supporting adult children, the child isn't allowed to fail because the parent either doesn't want their child to experience temporary discomfort or the parent doesn't want to admit that they, as parents, have failed. Regular payments start to feel like penance. When your child lacks the skills to limit their expenses based on their income, that's as much your failure as it is theirs. Guilt sets in. Checks are written. Nothing is solved.

I don't want my children to fail, but I look forward to their failures. They build character, resourcefulness, and guile. It's only when I try and mask their failures that their failures become my failures.

The entire discussion around cutting off an adult child can certainly ring of callousness. But your continued support of your adult children will ruin your financial life, and it will ruin their financial life. There are no winners. You believe you are sacrificing for another, but you aren't. You are the captain of a sinking ship.

One of the primary arguments used to justify this dangerous financial decision is the argument of relativity. You decide to help someone financially because you're in a relatively better financial situation than they are. It's a lose-lose situation. You make them more dependent on you as you head toward retirement. That math doesn't work.

I'd be remiss not to acknowledge scenarios in which financial support is not only warranted but necessary. Yet, these situations are the exceptions, not the rule.

The way out of your conundrum will be messier than you want. If you can't articulate to your child why your support is a problem, then that's where you begin by better understanding the impact of your entangled financial relationship. If your retirement plan is underfunded, you will work deep into your 70s so that your adult child can avoid understanding how money works.

Remember, your support of them isn't about the sacrifice of your money. It's much the opposite. This is about sacrificing your feelings and letting failure be the teacher.

Conclusion

Enabling adult children is a serious problem in parenting, and what makes it harder is that most parents aren't even aware that they are doing so. That is why you must train yourself to identify signs of enabling and know the difference between enabling your child and empowering them. The end goal is to make them able to take care of their life without your help. That doesn't take away your value in their life. Quite the contrary, it will only lead to a stronger bond with your children. Because one day, they will understand that all the times you didn't step in when they were struggling, it only made them stronger and more capable in life.

CHAPTER FIVE

DO SET BOUNDARIES, DON'T WAIVER

In the previous chapters, we discussed the importance of transitioning to a new approach to parenting when our children reach adulthood. This includes shifting parenting roles, listening to and understanding our children, and helping them become independent, wise, and responsible rather than enabling them. Now, we will focus on another important aspect of parenting adult children: setting boundaries. It's something that we mentioned briefly in the last chapter.

Setting boundaries can be challenging because it's not as simple as providing a list of acceptable behaviors. In this chapter, we will explore the various aspects of setting boundaries between parents and children. This includes the difficulties of setting boundaries, the importance of doing so, the best ways to set boundaries that benefit both parties, and many more factors that parents must consider when establishing rules and boundaries.

What does setting boundaries really mean?

Do you truly understand what it means to set boundaries? It may seem like a foolish question. It's not like this is some new concept in parenting. But it often happens that as parents, our understanding of 'boundaries' may not always be right.

Here are some common misconceptions about setting boundaries in parenting:

- It's not about making rules your children must follow at all costs.
- It's not about forcing your beliefs and what you think is right for your children.
- It's not about disciplining your children by telling them what they can and cannot do.

So if your idea of setting boundaries is similar to any of the above points, you need to reconsider. Basically, setting boundaries only applies to certain areas of the relationship between you and your children, and it's not a way for you to take control of their entire life. For example, you can't lay down rules and whom your children can choose as romantic partners. That's not something you can set boundaries on.

Setting boundaries with adult children means establishing clear and consistent limits around what is acceptable in the relationship between you and what is not. By setting boundaries, parents can help their adult children understand what is expected of them, protect their own well-being, and maintain healthy relationships.

You can set rules around when and how you will provide financial support to your adult children, such as only providing support in emergencies or only providing support if your adult children are actively working towards financial independence.

You can agree upon how often you expect to hear from your adult children and how you can carry out conversations and interactions with respect. For example, you can agree that both parties will not raise their voice or get agitated when there is a difference of opinion.

You can set boundaries as to when and where you are able to babysit or chauffeur the grandkids around. If your adult kids don't get along and can't be together, then set clear boundaries by scheduling family gatherings, so it's not so stressful and uncomfortable.

Establishing boundaries with adult children is an important aspect of parenting, even if it can be challenging. It is natural for parents to want to protect and support their children throughout their lives. But it is also important for parents to recognize that their children are now adults and need to be able to make their own decisions and take responsibility for their actions. By setting boundaries with adult children, parents can help them develop skills and independence.

Why is it challenging for parents to set boundaries?

Imagine going to your children, or calling them, and saying, "Hey, let's start following so and so rules," or "Listen, from today, we are going to set so and so limits." They give a nod of approval, and just like that, you've successfully set boundaries with your children. It's not that easy. Here are some reasons why:

1. Some boundaries you set may be very one-sided and only benefit you, not your children.

An example of a one-sided boundary that only benefits the parent might be a rule requiring your child to check in with you daily and report on their activities. This boundary can be one-sided because it only gives you a sense of control and reassurance. But it may not necessarily benefit your child, who may feel that their privacy is being violated and that they are being treated like children rather than adults.

This type of boundary is not healthy or sustainable in the long term, as it does not consider the needs or wants of the adult children and can lead to resentment and conflict in the relationship.

2. Parents might struggle to set boundaries if they cannot let their children go.

Boundaries and limits are not just meant to limit what your children can and cannot do but how they should behave. Because if that's how you see it, it becomes one-sided, just like the above example. Some boundaries should be there from your side, too, such as not interfering with certain life choices they make. You need to know when to let them go and exercise their freedom, when you should only serve as an advisor, and when it's justified to step up and intervene.

If you fail to give them freedom in many aspects of their life, you will also fail to set healthy boundaries that you and your children can mutually respect and agree upon.

3. Your child may not respect the boundaries immediately, or you may be inconsistent in enforcing them.

Not every child is a perfect human. Some children can be disrespectful and not acknowledge or follow your established rules. To make things worse, you might react harshly and further escalate the situation. Another problem is that some parents can be too lenient or inconsistent when implementing the rules that they have set. If you give your child some leeway every now and then, they will obviously develop the belief that your rules are flexible and don't need to be followed at all costs.

4. Parents may fear conflict with their children when setting boundaries.

I've personally heard many parents stressing over the fact that they're simply afraid of enforcing rules and boundaries on their children. They fear coming across as too strict and that their children might despise them, or it may cause conflict. So instead of communicating and explaining the importance of boundaries to their adult children, they just hold back and never develop the courage to set any rules in the first place.

5. Conflict between parents

Another common problem is that conflicts might arise between parents themselves. For example, you might be strict about not giving money to your child for unnecessary reasons, but your partner might do so silently without your knowledge. And in the case where the parents are divorced, there's an even greater disconnect, and the parenting patterns are all but cohesive. These situations happen quite often, where the other parent doesn't follow the ground rules laid down by one parent. If both parents are not on the same page with the implementation of boundaries, how can they expect their child to follow along?

6. Your child may be self-absorbed.

A self-absorbed child is one who's only focusing on themselves. They're always occupied with their work and ambitions, personal problems, etc. Now being self-absorbed isn't the same as being selfish. Selfishness is when someone only seeks their own benefit, regardless of how it may affect others. But a self-absorbed person is just someone unable to see things outside their own life.

Self-absorbed children may not necessarily oppose or disrespect your boundaries, but they are usually oblivious to the world around them, so they fail to understand the importance of boundaries set by parents. Making them realize and acknowledge your expectations and rules can be a tough challenge.

By bringing your attention to these difficulties, I'm not trying to discourage, demotivate or scare you. It's actually the opposite. Setting boundaries is a must when parenting adult children, but if you want to do it right, you also need to know about all the ways it can go wrong. So take your time to think and reflect upon these challenges and prepare yourself to face them when you work on establishing healthy boundaries with your adult children.

Where there is strife, there is pride, but wisdom is found in those who take advice.

— Proverbs 13:10

Why is it important to set boundaries?

As challenging as it is, you can't expect to have a respectful relationship with adult children without setting boundaries. Let's look at some key points that explain the importance of having well-defined, mutually agreed boundaries between parent and child.

1. It makes them independent

As children grow up and become adults, they need to learn how to make their own decisions and take responsibility for their actions. Setting boundaries allows adult children to make their own choices while still following acceptable behavior. You also start to limit financial support gradually. These changes support their independence and help them develop the skills they need to be successful on their own.

2. To maintain healthy relationships

Boundaries are essential for maintaining healthy relationships, which is no different when it comes to relationships between parents and adult children. By setting clear boundaries, you can help your adult children understand what is acceptable behavior and what is not. It gives clarity to your children regarding your expectations from them and allows you to understand what they expect from you. This mutual agreement and understanding strengthen and fosters the parent-child relationship.

3. To set a good example

As parents, you are role models for your children; this doesn't stop just because your children are adults. By setting and enforcing boundaries with your adult children, you are setting a good example for them to follow in their own relationships and showing them how to be respectful and responsible adults. It will also serve as a valuable lesson for your children to do the same when they have children of their own.

4. To keep yourself at peace

It is important for parents to remember that they, too, deserve respect. As a parent, you're not obliged to keep providing for or supporting your children every time. By setting boundaries with your adult children, you are making it clear that, in certain cases, they have to respect and accept certain decisions that you make, even if they may seem hard on them. And at the same time, your children also need to know that they now need to take care of their own needs, make their own decisions, and face their own struggles. You will always help them whenever they need your support and guidance with something important. But if they're always running to you for every little problem, it will also create disturbance and unnecessary stress in your life. So boundaries are essential for your own mental and emotional peace as well.

5. To help them become adults

Adulthood does not automatically come to all of us when we reach a certain age. When your children turn 18, they're 'physically' adults. But that doesn't guarantee mental and emotional maturity, and not everyone learns what it means to be an adult on their own. As adults, your children have to make important life decisions and bear the responsibility for their actions. Most importantly, they need to achieve financial independence and one day start a family and raise their own children. These are things that they slowly learn as part of their life experiences. And by setting boundaries, you are helping them learn such things one step at a time. Boundaries serve as lessons for your children on how to become mature and responsible adults.

One of my favorite authors, Lysa Tykeurst, writes in her book *Good Boundaries and Goodbyes:*

> Boundaries are for your sake and theirs, so you don't have to keep fighting against unhealthy behaviors, attitudes, and patterns. We can set a boundary, or we will set the stage for simmering resentments. Simmering in the frustrations of knowing things need to change, or trying to get the other person to change, is way more damaging than a boundaries conversation. Yes, boundaries can feel risky. But it's a much bigger risk to delay or refuse to have needed conversations.

Effective Strategies for Establishing Healthy Boundaries With Adult Children

Do you know what the toughest part about setting boundaries with adult children is? It's that you're not used to it. Let me explain.

Think about this. When your children were kids, you had authority over them to enforce rules. A child or a teen can nag, make a fuss, even throw tantrums and raise their voice in anger. But you didn't have to worry about them running away or cutting ties with you. They still needed you, and you won them over with a balance of strictness and affection.

But adult children may not feel obligated to listen to their parents. They won't just nod their head in agreement when you tell them to behave in a certain way or accept and follow certain boundaries. If you want to establish boundaries that you both mutually agree upon, you can't treat them like kids. So the reason many parents struggle in creating and implementing them, is because it can be awkward.. Now, you have to ask, explain, and discuss, which is a new approach for parents. Getting adult children to be on board with your expectations and boundaries may not be readily received, so it's important to learn how to do it in the best possible way without any conflict, unfairness, and resentment.

Keeping that in mind, I'm sharing some of the most useful and effective strategies that can help you set healthy boundaries and implement them cordially.

1. Communicate openly and honestly

All right, I know that 'communication' seems like the ultimate cliché when it comes to relationship advice. But that's only what people think. The truth is communication is and will always be the most important aspect of a healthy relationship. Marriages have fallen apart, and families have been ruined due to a lack of proper communication. So this is not something to ignore or roll your eyes over.

The first step towards setting boundaries with adult children is to just talk with them about this matter. Explain to them that they can no longer expect you to be behind them in all aspects of their life with the onset of adulthood. At the same time, make it clear that you will no longer interfere in all their choices, privacy, and personal space.

Now talking to them about boundaries doesn't mean that you have a one-time conversation, and a long list of rules will be active when the conversation ends. What it means is that you slowly discuss the idea of setting rules and boundaries with your adult child over the course of multiple conversations. Be direct and clear about your expectations and open to hearing their thoughts on the matter. Regular, honest communication is an excellent starting point before you lay down ground rules.

If you don't communicate: Your children might be thrown aback if you suddenly start throwing rules and boundaries at them without discussing things beforehand. It may be a lot for them to digest all at once, and they may end up keeping their distance from you instead.

2. Use natural consequences

If your children make mistakes, instead of getting angry at them or trying to rescue them somehow, let them learn through the natural consequence of their actions. Holding back is also an important boundary between a parent and an adult child. They should get the message loud and clear that you will no longer be their ultimate savior in every problematic situation.

This is also something we talked about in the last chapter. Covering up the mistakes of adult children or sheltering them from the negative result of their actions is one of the worst ways of enabling them. The parental instinct and urge to come to their rescue can be hard to resist but focus on the bigger picture. Facing the consequences in life makes them more alert in their life decisions. And it also makes them realize that as adults, they are not supposed to expect you to take care of their mistakes. Author C.S. Lewis wrote, *"Hardship often prepares an ordinary person for an extraordinary destiny."* Mistakes, failures, and poor choices may be necessary for true transformation and a life filled with joy and purpose.

3. Set limits on your involvement

It is important to set limits on your involvement in your children's lives and to recognize when it is time to step back and allow them to make their own decisions. Even the above point of letting your children face the natural consequences of their mistakes is one way of limiting involvement.

You also need to step back from all details of their personal lives, such as who they are friends with, whom they are dating, and their daily or regular activities. That's not to say you should be totally oblivious and never take an interest in what your child is doing. But the point is not to force yourself into their personal life. You don't get to have a say on things like whom they befriend, whom they date, where they want to work, etc. And you shouldn't even nudge them continuously to share all those details with you, at least not against their will. If your child is fine with letting you know about their colleagues, romantic partners, and other details of their life, that's great. If not, respect their privacy, too, just as you'd want them to respect yours.

This can be difficult, especially if you are used to being very involved in your children's lives, but it is important for their maturity and independence, especially when they become parents themselves. Jon and I learned this early on when grandkids came on the scene. There were many times when we felt they were being disciplined too harshly or the punishment didn't fit the crime. We would give Shawna "the look," letting her know we didn't approve. Well, that went over like a lead balloon. Of course, this made things worse. We brought condemnation on Mom and Dad and confusion to the grandkids. So boundaries were set for us not to intervene. If there was a concern, we would discuss it in private. Boy, was this hard, but we are not the parents, and eventually learned not to pass judgment or try to rescue the little darlings, who, in our eyes, could do no wrong.

4. Limit financial support

One of the biggest issues when maintaining boundaries between parents and adult children is when money is involved. Some parents are too emotionally attached to their children, so they can't say no when their child asks for financial support. In some cases, parents fear that their children will resent them or cut them off if they don't provide financial support. And sometimes, it's the child who feels entitled to their parent's money and keeps asking.

So you might need to toughen yourself up emotionally and mentally in terms of financial support. But it's more than just that. You also have an even more important role in helping them generate their own source of income. Help them look for jobs. Suggest them to learn a valuable, in-demand trade or skill. Discuss their plans and ambitions and guide them in starting their career early on.

These are just examples. You know your child best, so work with them to figure out how they can earn for themselves. For example, if they're still in college but want to move out of your home, why not help them find some part-time jobs? The bottom line is that limiting financial support doesn't mean you just stop giving them money and expect them to look for themselves. You also have to actively guide them towards financial independence and generating their own income.

5. *Take things slow, one at a time*

Even in previous chapters, we've often talked about making gradual changes. And the same applies to setting boundaries as well. You can't just decide to put forth a bunch of rules overnight or as soon as your child turns 18. In fact, you need to start establishing some basic rules and giving your children a little degree of freedom and independence as they reach their teenage years. And as they transition to adulthood, you can introduce one rule, one boundary at a time.

While they are still living with you, keep them accountable by either going to school, working or both. Make them get used to cleaning up after themselves and lending a helping hand with household chores. Discuss a timeline for when they should move out. Once they move out, you can decide what type of support you are willing to help them with and the best ways to communicate. The main point is that setting boundaries is a gradual process. As your child ages, you two have to decide together what works best and what boundaries need to be established over time.

Using these five simple and effective strategies, as well as a bit of discernment and common sense, it will be easier to set boundaries with your children. Of course, one important thing is to be consistent.

Additional Tips for Establishing Boundaries in Specific Situations

In some situations, it can be especially tricky or difficult, but even more important, to set clearly defined boundaries. I feel it's necessary to address these situations because they often happen with adult children.

- When an adult child is still living with you.
- When you don't approve of or get along with your child's partner or spouse.
- When your child is still immature, irresponsible, rude, and prone to making bad decisions.

I've put together some helpful tips for creating reasonable and healthy boundaries in each of these cases, based on personal experiences, the experiences of other parents, as well as suggestions and advice from professionals.

Boundaries with adult children living in your home:

Your adult child may have to stay in your house temporarily for various reasons. Maybe they are going through a tough time with no money and no place. Or maybe they are moving to a new location or moving from one job to another and need a place to stay for some time. It could also be that your child has just entered adulthood and will soon be moving out in a few months or so.

For all such cases when you have an adult child living with you, here are some boundaries you can set:

1. Agree upon a deadline for them to move out, and encourage as well as support them in finding their own place before the deadline.

2. If they can manage their own finances, ask them to pay a small rent and maybe contribute to the household expenses.

3. If they don't have any source of income, don't give them money. Instead, work out ways to help them get back on their feet financially by finding work. Most you can do is take care of their basic expenses for as long as they're staying, with a firm decision to cut off any support if they don't start earning for themselves soon.

4. Make the concept of "my house, my rules" clear to them. Bringing friends over frequently, heading out to party often and coming home late at night, making a mess in the house, and other unacceptable behaviors like these must not be tolerated in your home.

5. But along with all the rules, also give them the privacy they need. Even simple things like knocking before entering their room and not eavesdropping on their conversations with other people are important to show them that boundaries work both ways. They will appreciate that you respect their privacy and respect your rules in return.

Setting boundaries when you don't get along with your child's partner or spouse:

Let's not get into whether your child's partner or spouse is a decent person or the opposite. Regardless of what you think of them, the fact is that your child has chosen them as a partner, and you need to respect that. If it bothers you, the best thing to do is to reach a mutual agreement. Tell your child you're not exactly fond of their partner, so you wouldn't prefer being close to them, but they are both welcome during occasional visits and family celebrations.

There's nothing wrong with not getting along with or disliking certain people. We all have our own feelings and opinions about the people in our lives. But that doesn't mean we should express animosity towards them. Discuss this issue with your child and let them know how you feel, but also assure them that you won't act cold towards them as long as you keep your distance from their partner at most times.

At the same time, also introspect on your own feelings. Is your dislike towards the person based on reasonable factors, or is it just a matter of personal feelings and preferences? Maybe you just don't know them well enough, and your opinion of them might change if you try to interact with them. Be open to all these scenarios for the sake of your relationship with your child. If you've tried your best but still fail to like the person, it's best, to be honest with your child and avoid encountering their partner too often.

You don't need to feel guilty for not liking your child's partner. We all have people we like and dislike. It's a normal aspect of human nature. No harm is done as long as you don't act mean or spiteful. You can still act respectfully when they are around. They, too, may feel it necessary to establish boundaries with you. And that's ok.

Setting Boundaries with rude, disrespectful children and those that make bad decisions

As much as we love our children, not all of us can claim that they are angels. Humans are flawed, so our children also have their strengths and weaknesses. However, despite your best efforts in upbringing, sometimes your children grow up to be very rude and disrespectful. Send them a clear message that you will not sit down and digest every hurtful comment. However, never be rude from your end as well. One fire cannot be put out by another fire, so you need to act like water. Get your point across strongly but as politely as you can. You don't need to be loud and aggressive to make your voice heard. Try to reach out to them and figure out why they are hostile or disrespectful to you. Have you done something to offend them? Can something be done to mend the relationship and get along? Be passive and extend a hand of friendship. If their rude behavior has no valid reason and they are just stubborn and bitter, the best you can do is let them go.

One who is wise is cautious and turns away from evil, but a fool is reckless and careless.
— *Proverbs 14:16*

It's heartbreaking to watch your child make one poor decision after another. Maybe a toxic relationship, quitting school or a job or spending money irresponsibly. In worse cases, some may get into drugs or crime. If your children haven't gone down that path yet, do all you can to make sure they never do. But if they're already treading down the wrong path and are extremely difficult to deal with, you still need to establish boundaries with them. In fact, the importance of setting boundaries is even greater with such children. You can still try the previous points we talked about – communication, limiting financial support, limiting your involvement and letting them handle their own mess, and most importantly, facing natural consequences.

In fact, one of the main reasons children keep making some mistakes repeatedly is that parents don't let them learn their lesson the first time. And there's no better teacher than life itself. Let them get into trouble due to their actions and realize on their own what they have brought upon themselves. Let them face legal consequences if it's a serious case like involvement in a crime. If they have developed any drug addiction, confront them calmly and seek professional help and rehabilitation.

Many of us have or are dealing with a child caught up in drugs, alcohol, and/or criminal behavior. Depression among teens and young adults is at an all-time high, leading to greater substance abuse. Covid, the lockdowns, and forced isolation have been major contributing factors. Alcohol, pot, fentanyl, pills, and meth are all too familiar among the X and Y generations. Parents are struggling to know what to do and what not to do and grappling for help. Oftentimes, grandparents end up taking the grandkids if the parents are incarcerated or won't stop using. As a second-grade teacher for 22 years, I met several grandparents who were raising their grandkids. Most of them were doing the best they knew how, but also set boundaries with their adult children who were not allowed back in their lives without sobriety.

I almost lost my own daughter when she overdosed on methamphetamine at the age of 18. Her father and I knew she had a problem but didn't realize the extent of it. Shawna had lost weight, acted distant and rebellious, and had some questionable friends. The only thing I thought I could do was lock her in her room, and that wasn't an option. After rushing home from a busy weekend moving Karina back home from the coast, Jon and I found her in the ER of our local hospital. It was heartbreaking to see her: grayish skin, gaunt, unresponsive, and cold. An ambulance rushed her to the nearest children's hospital, three hours away. Because of a rare metabolic disease that she was born with, Shawna needed specialized care and treatment. Doctors, nurses, lab techs, clergy, and social workers, hovered about, in and out of her room for several days. I thank God for saving her. However, her reckless behavior didn't end when she was released. It took many more months of family counseling, setting boundaries, and tons of prayer. Shawna is now a wife, a mom of two teenagers, and a thriving, responsible adult who lives out her faith in God. Her life-changing experiences have given her a heart for others who struggle with personal issues.

Anger, fear, sadness, and helplessness can consume us. In these difficult situations, there are no easy answers, and boundaries can change from day to day. There's so much toxic behavior that we wonder if things will ever change. Lying, stealing, violent outbursts, and erratic behavior usually come with drug or alcohol abuse. I would recommend getting professional therapy for you, your adult child, and maybe the whole family. It's important to know that there are people who can come alongside you as you make decisions; don't enable and set clear boundaries. Getting involved with a local Al-Anon group will also give you support and direction. I have been involved with this organization for many years, dealing with addicted family members. The two things I learned were: 1. Only the addict can take steps to change and get clean. 2. The only one I can control is me.

Conclusion

With everything you learned about boundaries with adult children, the first thing to remember is that setting boundaries is not at all about controlling your children's lives. It's about drawing a line on your own personal space and well-being, your child's privacy as well, and keeping clear guidelines as to how the two of you expect to behave with each other.

Boundaries are important for your child's mental and emotional development, to help them become independent, and to maintain mutual respect between you. So follow the tips and strategies I've shared above, and above all, remember to be honest and patient, make gradual changes, and consistently enforce those boundaries at all times. When you and your child agree on some ground rules, your relationship is healthier and stronger.

CHAPTER SIX

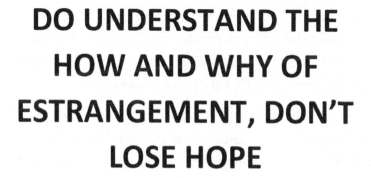

DO UNDERSTAND THE HOW AND WHY OF ESTRANGEMENT, DON'T LOSE HOPE

Your world can fall apart when your child tells you they no longer want you in their lives. Just the thought of being estranged from one's children can dishearten any parent. If that terrifying possibility becomes a reality, it will be any parent's worst nightmare.

Parents on good terms with their adult children may think something like this will never happen to them. But many of you may have experienced slight ups and downs in the relationship with your child, so you might want to be wary that things don't go from bad to worse. And maybe some of you are no longer in contact with your children, becoming estranged from them. Even in such cases, there is still hope.

No matter how good or bad things are between you and your child, the topic of estrangement, in general, is an important aspect of parenting that everyone must consider and be aware of. The purpose of this chapter is not to scare or dishearten you. I'm not trying to make you think your beloved children might cut ties with you one day. Instead, we are dedicating this entire chapter to estrangement because it's one of the most complicated issues that can arise between a parent and a child. But more importantly, as devastating as it may be, the truth is that this issue can be resolved. It won't be easy, no doubt, but it's very much possible.

So in this chapter, I'm going to detail the concept of estrangement between parents and children. We'll discuss the possible scenarios that can lead to estrangement and explore different reasons that lead to estrangement between parents and children. We'll even talk about all the pain and turmoil that parents experience when their children cut them off completely, and we'll focus on ways to cope with it and either mend the situation or move forward.

If your child has already detached you from their life, this chapter can help you.

If you feel like your child is drifting away and might completely cut you off someday, this chapter can help you.

But even if things are going smoothly, or at least okay, between you and your child, there is still a lot you can learn and implement from this chapter which will help you become an even better, loving, and understanding parent.

With that said, let's begin by considering a few basic things about the estrangement between parents and adult children.

Estrangement is Complicated

So far, we have discussed many important aspects of parenting adult children in the previous chapters. Lack of boundaries, being poor listeners, and enabling children –are all serious issues parents can face when dealing with adult children. But dealing with estrangement is the most complicated parental issue because nothing hits as hard as coming to terms with the fact that your child wants to sever all ties and end every connection between you and them.

Accepting that the child you loved and nurtured for years, for whom you made numerous sacrifices, now wants to cut you off completely –is undoubtedly one of the worst things a parent has to go through. Coping with it will be very painful, making it difficult to figure out what you should do next.

- Where did you go wrong? Why has your child taken such a drastic step?

- How can you deal with the pain and sadness?

- Can you consider the possibility of living the rest of your life without ever seeing your children?

Countless questions like these arise in the mind of parents when they become estranged from their children. If your child is married and has kids, it would mean that you won't be seeing your grandchildren either. So the more you think about it, the more complicated and chaotic things tend to be.

That's not to say that estrangement is the be-all and end-all of a parent-child relationship. But if you want to deal with it in the right way, you need to acknowledge how difficult it is and that you need to be strong enough to take proper steps.

Estrangement is Common

In 2020, a survey conducted by sociologist and Cornell University professor Karl Pillemer showed that 27% of Americans reported being estranged from at least one close family member or relative.

A similar survey was conducted in the UK back in 2014, where it was reported that 19% of participants had experienced estrangement from some family member.

A more recent survey by YouGov in 2022 had 11% of the participants cut ties with their parents.

Estrangement is a lot more common than we may think, and even more so in recent times. This increasing prevalence of estrangement between parents and adult children is worrying, and it calls for increased awareness among parents in this regard. One of the main reasons why more and more parents are becoming estranged from their children is that they don't realize how bad things are until it's too late. Considering how this issue is becoming quite common worldwide, parents must be cautious and adopt a proactive approach instead of a reactive one.

But Estrangement is Not the End of Your Relationship

If your child chooses to sever all ties with you completely, it's a huge decision. You'll probably try to reach out to them and apologize to them. But if they're adamant and refuse to reverse this decision, it may seem like it's the end of your relationship. Merely the thought of it is frightening.

And if some of you have already experienced this, I can only imagine the pain you must have endured. However, no matter how difficult it seems, there is a solution, a way forward. If you feel hopeless, the first step is to trust in God.

Have I not commanded you? Be strong and courageous. Do not be afraid; do not be discouraged, for the LORD your God will be with you wherever you go.   *— Joshua 1:9*

Let the Lord guide your thoughts and emotions, and let your faith give you the consolation you need to overcome the painful sadness. Because if you want to make things right, you need to make a fresh start with a new perspective. If you want to get in the right state of mind to mend an estranged relationship,

So before anything else, etch these words deep within your heart: *"Estrangement is not the end. There is still a way forward."*

Having said that, I'd also like to add that the 'way forward' doesn't always imply that you and your child will eventually reconcile. Sometimes, the best solution is to let go of them and continue living your life to the fullest.

So as the parent of adult children, you need to be clear about these three things regarding estrangement:

- It is more common than you may think.

- It is the most complicated and painful predicament a parent can experience regarding their adult child.

- But regardless of everything, it is not the end of your relationship.

What are the Reasons for Children to Become Estranged from Their Parents?

If you have become estranged from one or more of your children, you'd first want to know 'why.' Many parents quickly blame themselves when it happens, but that's not always the case. Many factors can lead to estrangement between parents and adult children, such as:

1. Difference in beliefs

One of the most common catalysts for parent-child estrangement is the difference in beliefs. Religious and political beliefs often cause conflict between parents and children, but it doesn't have to be just these two. Social beliefs can also be a topic of debate, as some parents may disagree with their children on topics of race, gender, or sexuality. Sometimes lifestyle differences create a rift between parents and children. For example, the parents might prefer a modest lifestyle, while their children might enjoy a thrifty lifestyle.

There's nothing wrong with having different beliefs and worldviews. The problem is when there is a lack of acceptance between each other's principles and ideologies. I think we've all seen or experienced conflicts caused by a difference in beliefs, be they big or small.

Initially, it starts with small debates as the child enters adulthood and starts forming their own ideas and views. Gradually, the debates turn into arguments, then the arguments get more and more heated, and before you know it, something hits the final nail in the coffin, and your child decides that it's best if they just shut you out of their lives for good.

2. Issues with your child's partner/spouse and in-laws

It's not uncommon for children to cut ties with their parents because:

- Either the parents didn't approve of their partner/spouse,

- Or the other way round, where their partner doesn't like their parents.

Again, this isn't a big issue, well, at least not unless both parties escalate things. We can't get along with every person we come across. So if you don't fancy your child's partner, there's nothing wrong with it. And if they have a problem with you, they are also free to feel that way. As adults, all parties involved – you, your child, and their partner – should be able to establish a mutual understanding without turning 'dislike' into 'hatred' or 'animosity.'

Failure to do so will leave your child in a tough spot. They will have to constantly play the role of peacemaker between you and their spouse, and if things get worse, they might be forced to choose between one or the other, which is why they may decide to cut you off.

Another possibility is the problem may not be with your child's spouse but with their in-laws, and it may get to the point where your child may decide that the only way to end the problem is by completely terminating your relationship with them.

So there are many ways in which issues between you and your child's spouse or in-laws can get quite ugly and compel your child to become estranged.

3. Overbearing parenting

Are you still trying to exert too much control over your adult children's lives? You may be doing so with the best intentions, whether to protect them, teach and guide them, or help them in any way. But if you're too worried about letting your children go even after they have entered adulthood, they might feel that you are overbearing. That is why we discussed many previous chapters about letting go of your children and changing your parenting role.

If you don't let your children make their own decisions as adults, they will slowly distance themselves from you. This gradual distancing can become complete dissociation over time, as they may decide it's best to stay away from you than to have you interfere in every aspect of their lives. Again, don't blame yourself or be too hard on yourself if you've unintentionally acted this way. But be careful and remember that despite meaning well for your child, overbearing parenting can slowly push adult children away until they decide to stay away forever.

4. Failure to listen

If your child has made it clear that they no longer want you in their lives, then obviously, they didn't make this decision overnight. And that means they must have dropped hints, even talked to you about it, that they are experiencing some troubles bonding with you. When parents fail to listen to their children, they also fail to see early signs of relationship barriers that could have been resolved with a little effort from both sides. And some days, children get tired of trying to get their parents to listen, so they just give up all hope.

If parents are not listening and always giving out unsolicited advice, it makes children feel unimportant, ignored, and unloved. And if such feelings keep growing in their hearts, they will slowly close themselves and eventually shut down completely by cutting off their parents.

5. Disagreement in Life Choices

Many parents find it difficult to approve their children's life choices in terms of career, social relationships, location, or any other major aspect of their lives. For example, a father may oppose his child's decision to drop out of college and try to become a YouTuber. A single mother may have dreamt of seeing her child take up medicine, only to discover that they want to pursue a career in sports. Parents may not agree with their children's decision to work and settle abroad. There are countless cases like this where an adult child's personal decision may not settle well with their parents.

At times like these, the severe reaction from parents can strain the relationship, which, in the long term, may gradually decline and lead to complete estrangement.

6. Separation of Parents

When parents go their separate ways, it's never easy on their children. And they often make things more difficult when they try to get the children to pick sides. It's not just hard but also extremely unfair to the children. Sometimes, the conflict between divorced parents can cause children to pick one over the other, and at other times, they may choose to avoid the hassle by cutting off both parents, even though it can be difficult for them to make that decision. They have their own lives, problems, and decisions, so they might not want to get involved in the feud between their divorced parents for their own mental well-being.

7. Toxic Children

In worst cases, the main reason for estrangement can be quite simple – some children are just toxic, especially towards their parents. I've heard many stories and witnessed many cases where adult children treat their parents terribly.

- They will never take responsibility for their mistakes and blame you for being a poor parent.

- They are nice to you when they need help or money and don't even acknowledge your existence at other times.

- They are never available for emotional support.

- They keep on making wrong decisions but never accept their faults.

These are just some signs to look out for in toxic children. So don't rule out the possibility that the reason why your child has cut you off is not that you did something wrong but because they are just a reprobate, irresponsible, and toxic person.

If you have an estranged child, perhaps you can figure out if these reasons are responsible for estrangement. If you're still a part of your children's lives, you should still be aware of these factors so you can take preventive measures and preserve your special bond with them.

How do you Deal with Estrangement from Adult Children?

The worst thing about dealing with estrangement is that, in most cases, it's unexpected and comes across as a shocking revelation for parents.

Maybe you're completely oblivious to how your child feels, that they are harboring feelings of resentment and are on the verge of dissociating themselves from you. Or maybe you are aware of some cracks in your relationship with them, but you think it's not serious enough to push them towards complete estrangement. Many parents even believe that no matter how much they fight and argue with their children, it will never break the blood bond and family ties between a parent and a child.

But when it happens, you get quite the shock. You might feel sad, anxious, or even angry, and it obviously isn't something you'll get over in a few days. However, sulking doesn't make things right. You have to pick yourself up and take some important steps to not just cope with estrangement but also to try and reconnect the broken bonds with your children. Dealing with estrangement takes a rational, well-thought-out approach.

I've put forth a simple 3-step system to deal with estrangement in the most appropriate manner to benefit both you and your child.

Step 1: Acceptance

As parents, we spend years and years living for our children more than we do for ourselves. We shower them with love and guidance and even make a lot of sacrifices to give them a good upbringing. Not all of us are perfect, and we all make mistakes, but we always have the best intentions. So if the same children we have loved dearly tell us one day that we are not a part of their lives anymore, it will be the most heartbreaking moment in the lives of every parent.

But the first step is to accept this fact, no matter how hard it is. Accepting means understanding that your child has taken this decision for some important reason. No child just wakes up one day and decides to stop talking to their parents forever. Maybe you were oblivious to some problems brewing in your relationship. Or maybe you were aware of some issues but didn't think it would be significant enough to compel your children to make such a huge and impactful decision. Many parents often believe that nothing can break the blood bond between a parent and child.

However, when the reality of estrangement hits you, it's unexpected. And the sudden revelation is hard to accept, which may cause you to enter a state of denial. You might try to keep calling your child to figure out what exactly happened and what you did and convince them to change their decision. Refrain from doing all these things. Accept that your child has made their choice, and they must have also done it after a lot of thinking. Even for children, it's not that easy to end their relationship with their parents.

So before you start overthinking the whats and whys or try to bombard your child with questions, you first need to take a step back and do nothing. Give your child some space, take some time for yourself, and accept that your child has made an important decision, which must not have been easy for them either.

Step 2: Stabilization

The next step is to stabilize yourself – mentally and emotionally – before taking action. Be patient and give yourself as much time as you need to clear your head and control your sadness and emotions instead of being controlled by them. Your mindset and emotions must be stable before you can take reformative actions.

Here are some things you can try out to cope with the pain and sadness of becoming estranged from your beloved children.

1. Seeking professional help

We're way past those ages when approaching a psychiatrist or therapist was shunned. Instead, you should be open to consulting a professional therapist to help you deal with your emotions. Sharing your feelings gives you an emotional outlet, and they can guide you in effective ways of dealing with sadness.

2. Let go of guilt

As we've already discussed earlier, estrangement can be caused by many reasons, and it's not always the parent's fault. So when your child severs connections with you, it does not necessarily mean you have been a bad parent. And even if it was something you did, feeling guilty about it will still do you no good. Letting go of guilt is vital.

3. Spend time on introspection and retrospection

Rather than sulking in sadness or feeling bad about your situation, spend more time analyzing possible reasons for estrangement. Look back at your own parenting decisions, try to see things from the perspective of your children, too, and talk to other close family members. All these things will shift your focus from heartache and despondency toward a more analytical and diagnostic approach.

4. Practice self-care

As much as you love your children and are hurt by being estranged from them, don't forget that you are worthy of love, care, and appreciation. And even if you're not getting that love from your children, you still need to practice self-love and self-care. When estrangement gets overwhelming, spend time on things you love instead. It could be anything you love, whether it is reading or cooking. Take care of your body, eat healthily, and keep taking good care of yourself both physically and mentally when you're in the midst of dealing with estrangement.

Remember the woman I met at a Bible study that was mentioned in Chapter 1? Here are some details that led up to the estrangement. Claudia was a single mom for many years. She did the best she could to raise three kids with no help from their father. When her son Tyler started high school, she noticed a change in his behavior and emotions. He didn't have the same set of friends he had in junior high. He became more and more distant and moved out when he was 18. Efforts to communicate and get counseling were made, but he made it clear that he wasn't interested. She knew Tyler was living a life that was contrary to the way he was raised, but she never judged him or made him feel unaccepted. Eventually, he completely cut off all ties with his family. A few years later, Claudia heard that he had a sex change operation and moved out of the country. Not a day goes by that she doesn't pray for Tyler. The pain and sadness are there, but she strives to be a loving mother and grandmother to her daughters and grandkids." Estrangement is real, and it hurts, but life must go on.

5. Spend time in refreshing activities and with good people

The best way to divert yourself from sadness is to go out with friends and loved ones. Plan a short trip, go on hikes or treks, or take a short vacation from work – activities like these will make you feel a lot better and take your mind off the tragedy and stressful thoughts. Spend more time with people who love and appreciate you, as they are a reminder that just because your child chooses to distance themselves from you doesn't mean you are a terrible individual.

The purpose of doing the things mentioned above is not to ignore your situation and move on or turn a blind eye to the problems brewing between you and your child. It's just to help you control the overwhelming sadness and distress so that you can become more rational and stable to take the correct steps for mending the estranged relationship.

Step 3: Reconciliation

Once you have spent enough time stabilizing your emotions, you'll be in a better state to take the necessary steps to reconcile with your estranged child. But be cautious because how you approach them can make or break things.

A huge mistake parents make when trying to reconnect with an estranged child is that they don't see the seriousness of the situation from the child's perspective. Surely, they didn't cut you off on a whim. It must have taken them a long time, and many factors built up month after month, year after year, until they finally decided that it was time to end things once and for all. And it must have hurt them too.

Seeing things from their perspective makes it clear that calling them and giving them one or two heartfelt apologies isn't enough to reconcile. Just as it took them a long time to cut ties with you, it will also take considerable time and effort to patch things up. With that in mind, you can follow a series of steps to slowly and gradually rebuild broken bonds and severed ties with estranged children.

1. Listen

Any reasonable adult child who cuts ties with their parents will not do so without giving valid reasons. In fact, they usually try to explain whatever is bothering them multiple times before making the extreme decision. So it's most likely that your child gave many hints during conversations, and you must have missed them. Maybe you noticed but shrugged them off. That is why it's important to listen and why we did an entire chapter about being better listeners.

Although it can be hard to realize that you could have preserved the relationship if you had listened on time, what's done is done, and you can't change the past. Instead, become a better listener now. Hear their reasoning behind choosing to cut ties with you. Understand what hurt them. And perhaps the most important part, listen without judgment. If you truly want to make things right with an estranged child, quietly hear their side of the story so you can identify the main cause of estrangement.

2. Reach out persistently but patiently

Of course, if you want to reconnect with estranged children, the first contact has to be from your side. When reaching out, don't make it too formal with something like an email. A personal letter or a heartfelt voicemail is much better.

The key is to be patient but persistent. They probably won't reply right away to your first message. Take some time before you reach out again. Keep trying, respect their silence, and give them space to think and reconsider.

3. Watch what you say when reaching out

When you're reaching out to estranged children, here are some things you should NOT do:

- Don't be desperate for their acceptance.

- Don't act defensive about your past actions.

- Don't try to justify, plead your case, or provide an explanation.

- But also, don't take all the blame and belittle yourself in the hopes that it will earn you forgiveness.

Instead, here are some things you should do:

- Offer them a genuine apology for whatever you said or did that hurt them.

- Tell them you're willing to move forward by finding common ground, especially if there are some differences in beliefs and life choices.

- Make it clear that you wish nothing more than to be united with them and that the door is always open from your end.

Reaching out is not the solution to estrangement. It is more of a means to let your child know that you still love them and desire to reconcile and that you are ready to do what it takes for it.

4. Be prepared to change yourself

All the above steps are pointless if you're not ready to make some changes from your end. You have to address the main cause of estrangement.

For example, let's say you were too dominating and intrusive on how your child should raise their kids, and that is why they decided to cut you off. If you want to reconcile with your child and see your grandchildren again, you have to stop interfering in how they parent their kids. Maybe you see your child taking the wrong parenting approach. Even then, you should let them handle their own family and learn from their own mistakes.

If you don't like their spouse, you still need to be nice and get along.

If you are religious, but your child is an atheist, don't try to persuade them, but love them. If the topic comes up, listen first, then share your convictions in a rational, understanding way.

These are just examples, but the point is you can't try to reconnect with an estranged child and then continue doing the same thing that pushed them away in the first place. To reunite with estranged children, you must address their concerns and change yourself.

Sometimes, It's Best to Just Move On

One of my friends had a daughter who had a history of substance abuse, could never hold on to a job for more than a few months, and was always coming back to her mother for financial support. Still, my friend tried her best to help her daughter correctly. She never gave money whenever asked but would try and set her up for small jobs here and there and always told her to get her life straight.

One day, the daughter called her up and said she needed $5,000 to bail out this guy she was dating. My friend flat-out refused, stating that it wasn't her problem and that she couldn't come up with such a big amount even if she wanted to. The daughter went into a raging fit, caused a huge ruckus over this matter, and vowed never to speak to her mother again. And she didn't.

After about three years of that incident, my friend heard from another relative that her daughter had eventually tied the knot with a decent guy and had just given birth to a healthy baby boy. She was heartbroken to hear this from a third person but still called her daughter to say that she'll visit to see her grandson. Her daughter bluntly said that she wouldn't allow her to come anywhere near the kid, so she'd only be wasting her time if she drove to the hospital. She hasn't seen her grandchild to date.

However, she has made peace with the fact that reconciling with her daughter may never happen, and she is content with her life now. Sometimes, the reason for estrangement is not the parent's fault but just a simple case of the child being toxic. In such cases, it's best for your own peace of mind to accept the situation and move on with life. Not being able to see your grandkids will surely be tough, but there's no denying that if your child is spiteful and vindictive, you are much better off keeping your distance.

Conclusion

Estrangement from children is one of the most tragic and distressing situations for parents. However, even in the worst cases, it's not always the end of your relationship with your child. It will take time, and it will be hard, but it's possible to reconcile with children who have severed ties with their parents. It requires three main steps: to accept the situation and the natural reaction of pain and sadness, to spend some time to stabilize your thoughts and feelings, and then to reach out and make amends with a fresh mindset.

But also remember that sometimes adult children can be completely irresponsible, spiteful, and don't want reconciliation. In such cases, it's better to move on and detach yourself from them, even though it's hard. Your health and emotional well-being are vital, so make connections with those who will love and encourage you. Never stop praying because miracles do happen.

CHAPTER SEVEN

DO TAKE TIME FOR YOURSELF, DON'T STOP BEING YOU

I trust that you have absorbed useful information and gleaned some valuable insight into your parenting journey from the previous chapters – shifting your role from a teacher and provider to a friend and guide, becoming a better listener, setting boundaries, avoiding things that enable your children, or even something as serious as dealing with estrangement.

While trying your best to be better parents, you're bound to feel some pressure and stress, both mentally and emotionally. And if you're overly preoccupied with such hardships and challenges, it will also affect your well-being. That is why parenting adult children requires you to focus not just on your children but also on yourself, which is going to be the crux of this chapter.

The experience of parenting adult children is not all rainbows and sunshine. If you're not taking time for yourself now and then, you'll cave in at some point. To become a better parent, you must have a sound mind and body. And above all, you need to stay strong in your faith because, despite all your aspirations and efforts, the will of the Lord prevails in the end. With these things in mind, let us explore the importance of self-care in the parenting context and look at various effective ways for parents to take care of themselves so they can fulfill their role effectively.

It's Common for Parents to Ignore Their Needs

After your children enter adulthood and eventually move out, it should give you more time to look after yourself, right? Because you're no longer in charge of them 24/7. At some point, you don't need to take care of their finances either. But many parents still lack that much-needed "me time."

Just think about your own life as a parent – when was the last time you stepped out of your parenting shoes and let yourself loose for a day of fun and relaxation?

Do you often get time to meditate, exercise, or even make time for some of your hobbies?

How long has it been since you last took a personal vacation with your spouse or friends?

These kinds of activities often become rare and occasional in the life of parents, even after their children embrace adulthood and move towards an independent life. Why does this happen? There are many reasons for the lack of personal time and self-care, such as:

Busy life

Juggling between job or business, daily household chores, financial management, future planning, and also being a guiding figure for their children, many parents barely get the time to focus on themselves amidst all the hectic responsibilities of a busy life.

Pressure and guilt

There is often an invisible pressure on parents to be the best version of themselves. We're always focusing on doing good for our children, even if it comes at the cost of our own happiness. So many parents feel guilty about taking time for themselves and think of it as 'selfish,' even though that's far from the truth.

Forced by habit

Children completely rely on their parents for care and support when they are young. That is why parents make many sacrifices for their children to get a healthy and wholesome upbringing in all aspects. When we spend 18 years (or perhaps more) living for our children more than for ourselves, it's obvious that such a lifestyle becomes a habit. And even when our children grow up and start living their own lives, this self-sacrificial nature remains within us, and we keep prioritizing our children more than our well-being.

Overbearing sense of responsibility

Many parents have a strong sense of responsibility towards their children and family. This is quite common in the case of people who had a tough childhood and didn't receive proper care, love, and support from their parents. Having experienced the hardships of being raised by irresponsible parents, they fear going the same route. As a result, they develop an overbearing attitude toward parenting and neglect their personal needs.

Usually, it is not a combination of some or all of these factors due to which parents either fail or choose not to take time for themselves. That is why lack of personal time and self-care is a lot more common in the lives of most parents.

Self-care is more important than parents realize

The benefits of self-care for your own well-being are quite obvious and common knowledge. It makes you healthy, happy, and able to live a more fulfilled life, but you probably already know these things. Instead, most parents fail to realize that it also helps you become a better parent and does wonders to flourish the bond with your children. Here's how:

Mental clarity for better decision making

In your parenting journey, you'll have to make many decisions from your head and not your heart. In other words, some of the most important decisions require a clear mind and a rational, analytical approach instead of letting emotions cloud your judgment.

Do you remember the previous chapters about setting boundaries or the negative consequences of enabling children? Those are perfect examples to highlight the importance of mental clarity in decision-making.

Your child wants a new car, and you can afford to buy one. But is it the right thing to do? The love in your heart may encourage you to make them happy by giving them what they want, especially when money is not a problem, but it requires a strong mindset to decide that you're not going to enable them. Instead, you'll help them work and earn the vehicle by themselves.

When your child is out of work and moves home, do you let them stay that way for as long as they like? Do you fear that confronting them in this matter will ruin your relationship? Your heart may tell you to be kind and loving towards your child. But again, it requires a strong mindset to set boundaries and speak the harsh truth that they can't just live a carefree life expecting you to look after them for however long it takes until they decide to get a job and move out one day.

There will be countless moments like these when you need to be strong-willed and make the 'hard' decisions for the betterment of your children. And that type of mental clarity can only be achieved when you consistently reflect on your mindset and get a hold of your emotions.

Emotional stability to become a strong support system

Connecting to the previous point, you also need to achieve emotional stability to become a reliable support system for your children. If you get easily distressed by the slightest hardships and challenges, how will you be able to console your children when they are stressed? How will you guide them when they need advice?

So if you want to support your children during difficulties, you need to be mentally and emotionally healthy. And for that, you need to take time for things like meditation, proper rest, and even good food. Worry, fear, stress, and many negative emotions result from chemical imbalances. Hormones such as cortisol, testosterone (in men), and estrogen/progesterone (in women) are responsible for our mood, feelings, and emotional states.

So you can't just 'tell' yourself to be happy, to stop worrying, and to be emotionally strong. Your diet, lifestyle, and physical activity all play a vital role in maintaining emotional stability. A hectic lifestyle with a severe lack of self-care will burn you out slowly, and you might become emotionally unavailable for your child without realizing it, which will strain your relationship in the long term.

Set an example for your children

When you practice self-care, you set an example for your children to do the same. And if they get better at caring for their needs, health, and emotional stability, they also achieve a fulfilled life. It's even somewhat ironic when you think about it. As parents, we often choose to sacrifice our well-being so that we can make our children happy. Yet, it only makes us more stressed and, in turn, makes our children stressed.

Instead, if we take time to care for our minds and bodies, we inspire our children to do the same, improving their quality of life. So if you want your children to be happy, stop trying to play a key role in every aspect of their lives. Rather become an example for them by being more kind and caring towards yourself.

Children look up to their parents, and if all they see is a parent who's always working, always worrying, and always trying to provide for others, they too might follow in the same footsteps. And when they have children someday, they'll prioritize everything above their well-being. It turns into an unhealthy cycle of life.

So when you think about it, practicing self-care has a greater impact not just on your life but on your children as well. This is because how you treat yourself sets an example for your children on how they should treat themselves.

Avoid unnecessary guilt and blame, and learn to let go

No matter how hard you try, you can't take care of your children's lives all the time after they have become adults. You are no longer the captain of their ship, only the first mate. So you need to understand that despite your best efforts, you're not responsible for everything in their lives. When your child gets into trouble or faces problems despite your advice and guidance, there's no point in blaming yourself. And still, we cannot help but experience some form of guilt when we see our children through difficulties.

So when such a situation arises, when something bad happens with your child, and you feel like blaming yourself, that's when it helps to take some personal time. Activities like meditation, exercise, and extra hobbies boost parents' physical, mental, and emotional well-being, making them more confident in their own abilities so that they can help their children in the right manner instead of feeling guilty and miserable.

Grow stronger in faith

Faith and action are both two sides of a coin. You can't just have faith but do nothing and hope that God will wave His magic wand. On the other hand, if you put all your effort into becoming a better parent for your child but still lack faith in God, your efforts will not bear fruit. So while you're doing your best to lead your children toward the right path and make them mature and independent, have faith that He is at work, no matter what things look like on the outside.

A key part of self-care is also to work on your spirituality by spending time in prayer and reading the Word of God. When you do that regularly, you will slowly but surely grow stronger in faith, which will bring abundant blessings, not just in your life but also in your children's lives.

To sum things up, parents who make time to take care of themselves enjoy a healthy relationship with their children as well because:

- They have a sound mindset to make better parenting decisions when dealing with their adult children, especially in difficult situations such as setting boundaries and avoiding actions that only enable their children.

- They have better emotional stability, so when the going gets tough for their children, they don't get distressed easily but instead become a strong support system.

- They set an example for their children to similarly take care of themselves and become responsible parents when they, too, have kids someday.

- They don't feel unnecessarily guilty or blame themselves for things they have no control of, especially in regard to their children's lives and decisions.

- They continuously strengthen their faith in God and fully trust in Him to guide their children on the right path as well.

And the opposite also stands true, which means a lack of self-care will sooner or later lead to undesirable scenarios such as:

- Making poor decisions as a parent due to a weaker mindset allows them to be manipulated by their children's desires.

- Getting stressed and worrying a lot when their children are in trouble and failing to console and support them.

- Setting a poor example of parenting for their children, who will most likely follow the same pattern and neglect their own well-being when they become parents one day.

- Feeling immense guilt over every little thing and often blaming oneself for being a bad parent.

- Losing faith in God, so they will stray further away from the heavenly peace that only comes through His grace.

All these points above highlight the simple fact that it's not just important but necessary for parents to take some time for themselves. And there's nothing selfish about it and no reason to feel guilty. Quite the opposite, caring for your well-being allows you to be more active, stable, reliable, and better equipped as a parent and role model. It helps you fulfill the roles required of parents of adult children – that of a trustworthy guide, a loving friend, and a wise mentor.

Tips for Parents to Practice Self-Care in all Walks of Life

I understand that a lack of self-care is not always intentional among parents. As we already discussed earlier, it's either the result of a hectic lifestyle that makes it nearly impossible to get some personal time or even when parents willingly choose to let go of their own needs. It's usually due to external factors such as societal pressure or force of habit after raising their kids for so many years.

But whether you're unable to make time for yourself or you're too concerned with caring for your children more than yourself, there's no denying that neglecting your welfare will only do more harm than good. That is why you must make a conscious decision and voluntary efforts to look after your own physical, mental, emotional, and spiritual well-being.

It's not going to be easy. Life will continue to be busy. Parenting will still bring its fair share of problems. The challenge is to make time for yourself amidst all these difficulties. We can help you by offering useful tips and advice regarding self-care in all walks of life.

Caring for Your Physical Health

Nowadays, there's plenty of information available online regarding different ways to boost one's physical health. So, without much elaboration, we'll quickly list a few pointers:

- Your diet should be your top priority, so ensure you are eating healthy meals to obtain all-around nutrition, giving the body health and vitality.

- Exercise. If you're too busy, start with short sessions a few times per day. There are plenty of "5-minute workouts" that you can find with just a Google search. My dogs are my alarm clock, so we are out the door at 5:30 A.M. for our morning walk. I also commit to an exercise class two days a week.

- Maintain a proper sleep schedule. Early to bed and early to rise is still an important and beneficial mantra to practice, even for parents! Getting seven to nine hours of sleep every night improves mental clarity, regulates blood sugar levels, improves the body's immune system and heart health, and helps to manage stress.

- Stay hydrated. This one's a no-brainer.

All in all, it's not such an arduous task to make these small changes. No need to hit the gym and sweat out your calories for 2-3 hours every day. If you can do that, even better. But at the very least, make sure you're just getting four basic things right: a nutritious diet, lots of water, lots of sleep, and some exercise every day.

Caring for Your Mental and Emotional Health

Again, when it comes to mental and emotional well-being, there are many effective strategies to follow where lack of time should not be an excuse.

Meditation

Spare 5 minutes in the morning, right after you wake up, and 5 minutes at night, right before bed. That's all the time you need to start making a habit of meditating. Ask yourself – is that too much to ask? A few minutes of breathing exercises and meditation at the very start and end of your day is perfect for keeping your mind clear.

Socializing

I usually recommend at least one social activity per week. In my opinion, that should be the bare minimum. You can grind through every day of the week and worry about your children and other life troubles, but at least keep one weekend to relax with friends and loved ones. Even a short night out where you grab a bite with friends is a great start. We are social beings at the end of the day. Companionship makes us happy and leaves us feeling fulfilled, loved, and appreciated.

Casual Time with Family

Every now and then, plan some casual activities with family. No rule of thumb here. It doesn't have to be every week or even every month. Invite your children over to dinner. If they're dating or married, you should obviously have their partner or spouse join along. It's also a part of socializing, but we're not mixing this with the above point because time spent with family means much more, especially to parents.

If everyone is busy, be the first person to initiate the idea of a small family get-together whenever everyone can arrange some free time. Maybe your children want to catch up too, but have just been too busy and keep putting it on hold. That's why you should not hesitate to approach them for some family time, whether it's dinner at home or some outdoor activity like brunch at the local eatery or a picnic.

Taking time for yourself doesn't necessarily mean you have to be alone. Spending casual time with the family is a great way to rejuvenate your mind from the daily pressures of life.

Healthy Mind in a Healthy Body

It's common knowledge that mental health also depends on your physical health. So when you eat and drink well, exercise regularly, and get proper sleep and rest, it helps to maintain optimum levels of testosterone or estrogen/progesterone and promotes other hormones like serotonin and dopamine, which can boost positive feelings like happiness, pleasure, and motivation. These hormones also prevent depression, anxiety, and stress. So the most effective way of boosting mental health and positive emotions is by maintaining a healthy lifestyle in general.

Communicating and Sharing with Loved Ones

One of the reasons why parents often face mental and emotional turmoil is when they keep all their feelings bottled within themselves. When there is no outlet for your emotions, it will eventually be too much to handle and lead to an outburst one day. So to avoid such a scenario, it's essential to have healthy emotional outlets. Communicate openly and regularly with your close relatives, your partner, and of course, your adult children as well. If any issues or problems are bothering you, share them with them instead of trying to deal with everything yourself.

Once again, the typical parental instinct makes us feel like we shouldn't burden others with our problems. But many people love and appreciate you and are eager to help you out, be it by offering solutions to certain troublesome situations or simply by lending you their ears so that you can just share your thoughts and feelings, pour your heart out, and feel a bit lighter. Don't isolate yourself. Seeking support and consolation from loved ones does not burden them. In fact, it makes them happy that you trust them and share your mind and heart with them. And, of course, it provides a means to release your pent-up emotions healthily.

Spend time indulging in hobbies

A simple and easy way to release stress and have a relaxing, pleasant time is to indulge in any hobby you enjoy. Or you can even develop new hobbies that you haven't tried before. Maybe you've wanted to try gardening for a long time. Or you could try something as simple as journaling. Some hobbies, like swimming or learning a new skill, can be quite productive. Doing such activities now and then will be a refreshing break from the monotonous circle of life and leave you feeling rejuvenated.

Professional support

If you face higher mental stress that doesn't seem to go away by any of the above methods, seeking professional support might be the best option. Don't hesitate to approach a therapist. There's a reason they are professionals and are good at what they do. When all other options fail to provide relief, talking to a therapist will be immensely helpful for you to address the reasons that are making you sad and stressed. They will also help you figure out the right course of action to break away from your mental state and embrace a happier state of mind. I, for one, never even considered seeing a therapist. However, when I suddenly found myself in "uncharted waters" as a widow, seeing a therapist has been a Godsend!

Caring For Your Spiritual Health

The final piece of the puzzle for personal care is to focus on your spiritual health. To improve the state of your spirituality and become stronger in faith, here are some things you can do:

1. Spend time in personal prayer and reflection.

Do not be anxious about anything, but in everything by prayer and supplication with thanksgiving let your requests be made known to God. — *Philippians 4:6*

Continue steadfastly in prayer, being watchful in it with thanksgiving. — *Colossians 4:2*

Prayer is the foundation of building a personal relationship with God. He knows you, loves you, and wants you to come to Him just as you are, no matter what you're going through, good or bad. Be open and honest, laying down all your heart's desires to the Lord. He is faithful, and we can trust His perfect will.

2. Read the scripture regularly.

Like prayer, another essential part of growing spiritually is reading the scripture daily. The Bible contains wisdom to guide us in our way of life, consolation to ease our sorrow during difficulties, and motivation to keep living a righteous life. Just like food nourishes the body, the Word of God nourishes our souls. Without it, you will be spiritually hungry and unfulfilled in life. But when you consume scripture daily, you will gain wisdom and peace beyond your understanding. Part of my morning routine is to read a daily devotional that gives me strength and encouragement for the day.

3. Put your faith into action

Faith is not true if it doesn't convert to action. Be kind and humble as a parent. When your children make mistakes, do not get agitated or give them the "I told you so" treatment. Practice patience in adversity, and ask the Lord to guide you and your children. And most importantly, when you feel low or lonely during hard times, know that God is with you and there is nothing you should fear. Unwavering confidence and trust in God is a true testament to your faith.

Trust in the Lord with all your heart, and do not lean on your understanding. In all your ways acknowledge him, and he will make straight your paths.   *— Proverbs 3:5-6*

All these points above are proven effective for parents in boosting their physical, mental, emotional, and spiritual well-being. But one last thing to keep in mind is that you should introduce self-care activities in your busy life at a slow and steady rate. Take small steps each day. Make time for little changes one by one. Also, begin by spending just a few minutes of self-care each day.

Conclusion

We have discussed a lot of important topics about parenting in this book. Every chapter has covered a significant aspect of parenting in great detail. There's no doubt that if you want to guide your adult children on the right path, you must implement everything you have learned. But in doing so, it's easy to get too caught up in your role as a parent and forget about your role as an individual who also needs to pay attention to your own needs. As such, it's only reasonable that this final chapter also emphasizes your personal well-being.

So while you're busy changing your parenting approach and empowering your adult children, don't forget to show yourself some much-needed love, care, and appreciation. At the end of the day, despite all your efforts, the best thing you can do is take some time for yourself and leave everything in the hands of the Lord.

CONCLUSION

Parenting adult children is a rollercoaster ride. There are difficulties and challenges, but also a lot of love and affection. You want what's best for them, but you also must let them decide what's best for themselves. And at times, it will definitely make you question your own ability and discernment as a parent.

So amidst all those emotions, confusions, and good intentions, I hope this book has helped you clarify your role as an adult child's parent. As we wrap things up, let us quickly recap everything we discussed and learned as we journeyed together through every page and chapter of this book.

- Be aware of the new generation mentality. Don't expect your children to perceive the world the way you do. Realize that the modern world has changed drastically with technology, cultural shifts, social media, etc. To be a better parent, you have to understand their way of thinking and the culture and lifestyle of the new generation.

- Adjust your role as a parent. Come to terms with the fact that you are no longer their sole provider and the one to make decisions on their behalf. Let them pave their way, but always be a mentor to guide them and a friend to encourage them and nudge them in the right direction.

- Be a patient listener. They've listened to your words and wisdom throughout their childhood and teenage years. Now it's your time to listen to their opinions, views, and ideas. When you talk less and listen more to adult children, you get clear insights into what is on their minds and heart, so you can offer the right advice when asked or just become a good friend to them that lends an ear when needed.

- Don't enable your children. Doing things for them out of love, which only makes them dependent or entitled, is a huge mistake. Instead, teach them how to solve their problems, make tough decisions, and lead an independent, respectable life through their hard work and efforts.

- Set clear boundaries, and ensure you and your children respect them. Treat them like the adults they are, and establish ground rules on what is okay and what isn't in your relationship. Whether it's limiting financial support or setting fixed times for communicating, boundaries teach your children to become independent and for you and them to respect each other.

- If you have estranged children, know that it is not the end of your relationship. First, get a hold of your own sadness and disappointment. Then with a fresh mind, you can try to gradually resolve the issues that led to estrangement and attempt to reestablish your bond with them. In some cases, you should also be willing to accept that maybe the best decision is to remain estranged from children who fail to respect their parents and become responsible adults.

- And in the end, after all is said and done, do not forget to take care of your own well-being. Don't ignore self-care while you're too busy being a good parent. In fact, taking care of oneself is also an important responsibility of a parent so that they can set an example for their children to do the same.

Remember that these are intricate aspects of parenting that cannot be practiced and implemented overnight. You know your kids, their personalities, strengths, and weaknesses. Every family is unique, and family dynamics change throughout the years. Keep everything you learned deep within your mind and heart, and enjoy the journey of parenting one day at a time while striving to change your approach and do the right thing for your children each day. God bless you.

REFERENCES

CHAPTER ONE

Brown, S. (2019, April 3). *Difference Between Gen X And Gen Y | Difference Between.* Difference Between. http://www.differencebetween.net/miscellaneous/difference-between-gen-x-and-gen-y/

Greer, J. (2022, April 4). *When Adult Children Don’t Share Your Values.* Focus on the Family. https://www.focusonthefamily.com/parenting/when-adult-children-dont-share-your-values/

Social Media and Mental Health: What are the Positive and Negative Effects? (2021, November 5). Montare Behavioral Health | Mental Health Treatment in Los Angeles. https://montarebehavioralhealth.com/social-media-and-mental-health-what-are-the-positive-and-negative-effects

CHAPTER TWO

Rainey, D., & Rainey. (n.d.). 10 Ways to "Let Go and Don't Control" Your Adult Children. The Raineys | an Outreach of CRU. https://www.theraineys.org/post/10-ways-to-let-go-and-don-t-control-your-adult-children

What to do when your grown child resents how you parented them. (2019, August 14). NBC News. https://www.nbcnews.com/better/lifestyle/your-adult-child-resents-way-you-parented-them-here-s-ncna1042081

Brooks, A. C. (2022, November 17). A Path to Harmony for Parents and Their Adult Kids. The Atlantic. https://www.theatlantic.com/family/archive/2022/05/parents-adult-children-lower-your-expectations/629830/

CHAPTER THREE

5 Tips to Help Parents Be Better Listeners | Social & Applied Human Sciences. (n.d.). https://csahs.uoguelph.ca/news/2022/01/5-tips-help-parents-be-better-listeners

Stoltzfus, J. (2021, February 19). Parents – Learn to Listen More Effectively to Your Young Adult. Parents Letting Go | Dr. Jack Stoltzfus. https://parentslettinggo.com/parents-learn-to-listen-more-effectively-to-your-young-adult/

Cooper, A. (2022, August 24). How to Talk WITH — Not AT — Your Adult Children. HowStuffWorks. https://lifestyle.howstuffworks.com/family/parenting/parenting-tips/how-to-talk-with-adult-children.htm

Admin. (2020, August 31). Lesson for Parenting Adult Children: Be Careful about Giving Advice. The Legacy Project. https://legacyproject.human.cornell.edu/2020/08/31/lesson-for-parenting-adult-children-be-careful-about-giving-advice/

CHAPTER FOUR

The Dangerous Effects Of Parents Enabling Grown Children | ReGain. (2023, January 18). https://www.regain.us/advice/parenting/the-dangerous-effects-of-parents-enabling-grown-children-2/

Graves, K. (2020, July 16). 6 Steps to Stop Yourself from Enabling Grown Children. Crosswalk.com.

https://www.crosswalk.com/family/parenting/steps-to-stop-yourself-from-enabling-grown-children.html

How To Stop Enabling Grown Children And Why It's Important | BetterHelp. (2022, October 7). https://www.betterhelp.com/advice/family/how-to-stop-enabling-grown-children-and-why-its-important/

Attaway, J. J., & Anderson, D., Ph.D. (2022, October 18). Supporting vs. Enabling. Child Mind Institute. https://childmind.org/article/supporting-vs-enabling-a-child-with-challenges/

Laufik, M. (2019, September 3). 6 Signs You're Enabling Your Grown Child (and How to Stop). PureWow. https://www.purewow.com/family/how-to-stop-enabling-your-grown-child

CHAPTER FIVE

Lovering, N. (2022, August 9). Setting Boundaries With Your Adult Children. Psych Central. https://psychcentral.com/relationships/boundaries-with-your-adult-children

Kreiczer-Levy, S. (2019). Parents and Adult Children: The Elusive Boundaries of the Legal Family. Law &Amp; Social Inquiry, 44(2), 519–525. https://doi.org/10.1017/lsi.2019.19

Bernstein, J., Ph.D. (2020, December 9). How to Deal With Disrespectful Adult Children. Psychology Today. https://www.psychologytoday.com/us/blog/liking-the-child-you-love/202012/how-deal-disrespectful-adult-children?eml

Bernstein, J., Ph.D. (2022, December 28). Setting Boundaries With Your Self-Absorbed Adult Child. Psychology Today. https://www.psychologytoday.com/us/blog/liking-the-child-you-love/202212/setting-boundaries-with-your-self-absorbed-adult-child

Dad, A. P., & Dad, A. P. (2020, May 27). 10 Ways to Establish Clear Boundaries for Children. All Pro Dad. https://www.allprodad.com/10-ways-establish-clear-boundaries-children/

CHAPTER SIX

Pillemer: Family estrangement a problem 'hiding in plain sight' | Cornell Chronicle. (2020, September 10). Cornell Chronicle. https://news.cornell.edu/stories/2020/09/pillemer-family-estrangement-problem-hiding-plain-sight

Orth, T. (2022, December 20). All on the family: ties, proximity, and estrangement. YouGov. https://today.yougov.com/topics/society/articles-reports/2022/12/20/poll-family-ties-proximity-and-estrangement

Coleman, J. (2022, July 28). Why Parents and Kids Get Estranged. The Atlantic. https://www.theatlantic.com/family/archive/2021/01/why-parents-and-kids-get-estranged/617612/

Cuppy, C. (2022, March 31). Family Estrangement: 6 Ways to Reconcile with Adult Children. Focus on the Family. https://www.focusonthefamily.com/parenting/family-estrangement-6-ways-to-reconcile-with-adult-children/

O'Dair, B. (2022, August 24). How to Reconcile With Your Estranged Adult Child. AARP. https://www.aarp.org/home-family/friends-family/info-2020/estranged-child.html

Holmes, M. (2022, December 9). How To Reconnect With An Estranged Adult Child. HuffPost. https://www.huffpost.com/entry/how-to-reconnect-estranged-adult-child_l_63920829e4b0169d76d4f3ae

CHAPTER SEVEN

Lcsw, A. M. (2020, January 31). 15 Self-Care Strategies for Parents. Verywell Family. https://www.verywellfamily.com/self-care-for-parents-4178010

Burton, N. (2020, November 2). Self-Care Strategies for Parents When You Have No Time for Yourself. Healthline. https://www.healthline.com/health/parenting/self-care-strategies-for-parents-no-time

Prvulovic, T. (2023, January 24). How to Stop Worrying About Your Adult Children. Second Wind Movement. https://secondwindmovement.com/worrying-adult-children/

Swamy, A. (2021, December 21). Are your mind, body, and spirit in sync? Here's why self-care is important for parents. Shri Harini Media Ltd. https://www.parentcircle.com/selfcare-tips-for-parents/article

Made in the USA
Las Vegas, NV
14 December 2024

14242822R00089